W9-BCR-898

A Wife in Musashino

MICHIGAN MONOGRAPH SERIES IN JAPANESE STUDIES
NUMBER 51

CENTER FOR JAPANESE STUDIES
THE UNIVERSITY OF MICHIGAN

895.635 O1w
¯Ooka, Sh¯ohei, 1909-
A wife in Musashino

SEP 2005
Received
Ohio Dominican

A Wife in Musashino

Ōoka Shōhei

TRANSLATED WITH A POSTSCRIPT BY DENNIS WASHBURN

CENTER FOR JAPANESE STUDIES
THE UNIVERSITY OF MICHIGAN
ANN ARBOR   2004

Copyright © 2004 by Dennis Washburn

All rights reserved

Original Japanese Text *Musashino fujin* Copyright © 1950 by Shōhei Ōoka

JLPP

This book is published within the Japanese Literature Publishing Project managed by the Japan Association for Cultural Exchange on behalf of the Agency for Cultural Affairs of Japan.

Published by the Center for Japanese Studies,
The University of Michigan
1085 Frieze Building, Ann Arbor, MI 48109-1285

Library of Congress Cataloging in Publication Data

Ōoka Shōhei, 1909–
    [Musashino fujin. English]
    A Wife in Musashino / Ōoka Shōhei ; translated with a postscript by Dennis Washburn
    p. cm. — (Michigan monograph series in Japanese studies ; no. 51)
    ISBN 1-929280-28-9 (alk. paper)
    I. Washburn, Dennis C. (Dennis Charles), 1954– II. Title. III. Series.

PL835.O5M813 2004
895.6'35—dc22

                                                                    2004062814

This book was set in Goudy Old Style.

This publication meets the ANSI/NISO Standards for Permanence of Paper
for Publications and Documents in Libraries and Archives (Z39.48–1992).

Printed in the United States of America

CONTENTS

NOTE ON JAPANESE NAMES AND PRONUNCIATION

I have followed the Japanese custom that places the family name (the surname) before the given or personal name (thus Miyaji Shinzaburō, Akiyama Tadao, or Ōno Eiji instead of Shinzaburō Miyaji, Tadao Akiyama, or Eiji Ōno). This custom is perhaps familiar to English-speaking readers, but it deserves mention here because Miyaji, Akiyama, and Ōno are for the most part identified in the novel by their family names. In contrast the main female characters, Michiko and Tomiko, and Michiko's male cousin, Tsutomu, are invariably identified by their personal names.

Names are presented as they appear in the original text because the family name clearly marks a difference in social and legal status. The use of the family name as a marker of status is exemplified by the character Ōno Eiji. Generally he is called Ōno, even by his wife, Tomiko. However, in certain passages that describe his life before he was married, or in passages where some intimacy in address is appropriate, he is referred to as Eiji.

I have resorted occasionally to redundant identification for certain place names. For example, Tamagawa means "the river Tama," but for its initial appearance in the text I identify it as the "Tamagawa River." In subsequent appearances I simply use "Tamagawa" because that reflects common usage in Japan.

There are five vowels in Japanese, and their pronunciation corresponds roughly to the pronunciation of Spanish or Italian vowels. When a line appears over a vowel, it is lengthened—thus ō is pronounced "oo". An apostrophe is used to mark breaks between syllables that otherwise might be ambiguous when written in Romanized script.

Consonants are pronounced roughly the same as English consonants. G is always "hard," as in "got." *Ts* is like the "ts" in "tsetse fly" or in "let's." The Japanese *r*, whether medial or initial, is ever so slightly trilled and its sound may fall somewhere between an "l" and a "d" to the ear of a native speaker of English.

The basic units of Japanese words are syllables, which may consist of a single vowel, a consonant-vowel pair, a consonant-vowel trio (two consonants and a vowel), or the nasal final consonant -n, which appears only at the end of words. Except for final -n, all syllables end in a vowel. Thus, the place name Hake, for example, is pronounced as two distinct syllables, Ha/ke. Syllables receive equal stress, so intonation is relatively flat and even.

The text I used for this translation is the revised paperback edition published in 1999 and reprinted in 2002 by Shinchōsha.

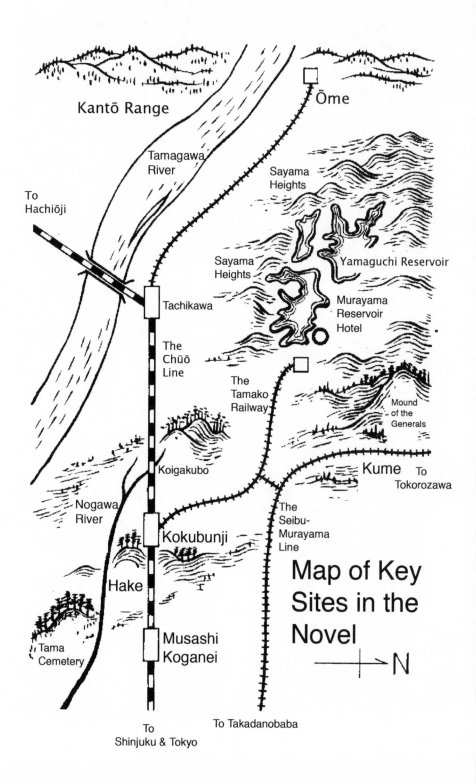

Kantō Range

Tamagawa River

To Hachiōji

Sayama Heights

Sayama Heights

Yamaguchi Reservoir

Ōme

Tachikawa

The Chūō Line

The Tamako Railway

Murayama Reservoir Hotel

Mound of the Generals

Koigakubo

Kume   To Tokorozawa

Nogawa River

Kokubunji

The Seibu-Murayama Line

Hake

Map of Key Sites in the Novel

N

Tama Cemetery

Musashi Koganei

To Shinjuku & Tokyo

To Takadanobaba

A Wife in Musashino

Are feelings such as those that stirred the heart
of the Countess d'Orgel out of fashion?

— Radiguet

Chapter 1

The People of Hake

People who live in the area aren't sure why the place is called Hake. But mention the name of Ogino Chōsaku, whose family is one of the oldest of the many Ogino households among the farmers of this region, and they assume that Hake is the elevation where Chōsaku's house is located.

There is a road that runs from the tracks midway between the Kokubunji and Koganei stations on the Chūō line. If you walk south along that road for about two blocks, crossing some level fields, the terrain suddenly descends and opens out onto the basin of a small river called the Nogawa. The slope of the narrow current is relatively steep because the basin is one of the oldest terraces created when the ancient Tamagawa River shifted to the southwest. In an earlier geological age the Tamagawa flowed out from the Kantō highlands, producing the sedimentation that shaped the broad Musashino plateau. This plateau is now bounded on the north by the rivers Irumagawa and Arakawa, on the east by Tokyo Bay, and on the south by the present-day Tamagawa.

The far bank of the Nogawa, with its narrow rice paddies, rises gently to form a shield-shaped plateau dotted with pines, mulberry trees, and factories. At Fuchū the land descends further into the basin of the Tamagawa, forming a second terrace. The Nogawa is one of the many vestigial rivers the ancient Tamagawa left behind on the plains of Musashino. Its terrace passes through Mitaka, Jindaiji, and Chōfu and emerges in the Tamagawa basin just above Kitami. A little further downstream the Nogawa merges with the Tamagawa, which continues on toward the Tama Heights in Kanagawa, meandering as far as Rokugō.

The large zelkova and oak trees that tower conspicuously over this heavily forested slope are likewise vestiges of the virgin forest of ancient Musashino. One of the zelkova that grew near Chōsaku's house on Hake was instantly recognizable even at a distance. Some say that the name "Hake" is either the pronunciation in the local dialect of the word for nose, *hana*, or that it is a word meaning "edge" or "rim." Those etymologies were probably derived from the spot beside that landmark zelkova where a small elevation with stone steps rises from a road that threads the skirt of the slope. However, it is more likely that Hake simply means "ravine." The name refers not to

3

the place where Chōsaku's house is located, but to one of the hollows cut deep into the slope, reversing the flow of the water that drains near the road west of the house.

Water gushes out where the interior of the hollow gradually rises and becomes a low cliff. The sandy stratum that lies beneath the reddish loam of Musashino is exposed there. Clean subterranean water bubbles forth as though crawling out of the earth and quickly becomes a murmuring stream starting its downward flow. Chōsaku's family built a small pool where this stream crosses the lower road and use it to wash vegetables from the fields.

Because of the abundance of spring water, this slope has been inhabited from ancient times, when Musashino was covered by dense virgin forest, to more recent times, when Musashino was transformed into a vast, wild plain where thirsty travelers perished. No doubt Chōsaku's ancestors first settled at Hake because of the presence of this spring, and over time they became known as the Oginos of Hake. Nowadays, with the development of drilling techniques, private wells are common and there is less need for the spring water. Thus, people have come to think that Hake refers only to the sunny elevation where Chōsaku's house now stands.

There are of course other reasons, apart from changes in lifestyle, why people have forgotten about the spring. For one, a hedgerow now runs along the entire width of the hollow just twenty meters to the west of the pool used by Chōsaku's household, blocking the hollow from view. Flowering trees—plum, osmanthus, evergreen magnolia—blossom throughout the four seasons just inside the stylishly roofed hedgerow gate, indicating that the house is the residence of one of the increasing numbers of urban dwellers who have moved to this area in recent times. Looking at it from the road, passersby have no idea that beyond the hedgerow is a spring that was once the source of the region's prosperity.

Thirty years earlier a parcel of land in the hollow measuring about four thousand square meters fell for practically nothing into the hands of a Tokyo bureaucrat named Miyaji Shinzaburō. This parcel contained the spring, and so Chōsaku's father set some strict conditions on the transfer, retaining the rights to use the water in the spring pool by the road and charging for the expense of digging a new well on the grounds of Hake. Even with these conditions, Chōsaku's father grumbled constantly until the day he died about the loss of the land. And he had reason to complain, because the station at Koganei, a mere fifteen-minute walk from Hake, was constructed just five years after he let go of the parcel, which subsequently tripled in value.

Miyaji was an official in the Ministry of Railways, and so of course he'd had inside information on the construction of the new station. To be fair, his decision to buy the parcel was not motivated solely by financial interest. He was genuinely fond of Hake because he loved places that had water and that were sunny and warm. Most pleasant of all was the view of Mt. Fuji from there.

Fuji appeared small in the distance beyond the Tanzawa mountain range, which thrust up like a promontory overlooking the far side of the Tama basin and the Sagami plain. Miyaji never tired of watching the transformations of Fuji's appearance, which changed according to the seasons and the weather. He also loved the forest, and he had various unusual ornamental trees planted on land that was already heavily wooded. His house had been built on a lot cut into the hillside on an elevation level with the spring, and he set the new trees close to the eaves so that their leaves would never obscure his view of Fuji.

Miyaji Shinzaburō loved Mt. Fuji so much because he had spent his childhood years within sight of it. His family had served as *hatamoto*, direct retainers to the shogun. Their fortunes collapsed following the dissolution of the shogunate in 1868, and Miyaji was born soon after they moved to Shizuoka.

It was a severe handicap to have to return to Tokyo as a member of a family stigmatized by service to a ruined lord. Only after passing through many hardships did Miyaji manage to land a job in the Meiji government. As the characters for his name, Shinzaburō, indicate, he was the third of five brothers. His siblings had all scattered during the turmoil of the early Meiji period, and by the start of the Taishō period the only one of them with whom he was corresponding was his youngest brother Tōgo, a soldier who had risen to the rank of colonel. Tōgo committed suicide with a pistol the day after the surrender of the Imperial Army in 1945, and with his death Shinzaburō became the sole survivor of the Miyaji family, once prosperous *hatamoto* with an annual stipend of 2,500 bushels of rice.

Miyaji said his brother Tōgo was a fool. In his opinion, the recent defeat was the inevitable outcome of the recklessness of the foot-soldier government of the Meiji period. To have followed such a government was inexcusable. Miyaji himself was an avid reader of Katsu Kaishū, and he often bewildered his guests by exaggerating the progressive nature of the plans of the council of feudal lords drawn up by centrist men of talent like Katsu near the end of the Tokugawa period. He would say that a defeated Japan would now finally return to the rationalism of the age of Tokugawa Ieyasu.

Miyaji was viewed as something of an eccentric during his service in the bureaucracy. He despised the government he worked for, but he was clever when it came to making money. By the time he reached retirement age at the end of the Taishō period, he had already accumulated a substantial estate. Even after he retired he made use of his connections, serving for two years as director of a privately owned railway in Shizuoka. He further increased his fortune during those two years, then moved permanently to the house at Hake, which he had built earlier as a country residence.

In this way he had achieved a measure of happiness. His children, however, were not as fortunate. His wife, Tamiko, was also born into a former samurai household in Shizuoka prefecture. She had three children, two sons and a daughter. Both sons died as young adults, leaving only the youngest child, Michiko. Michiko was married before the second son died, but because she had no children the Miyaji family was left without an heir. This turn of events did not especially trouble Miyaji, whose own life had been an adventurous climb in the world. When the excavations for Miyaji's house at Hake were begun, a grave that had been dug into the face of the cliff was uncovered. It contained human bones, which Tamiko took as a bad omen. She insisted that construction be halted and a different site chosen. Her husband wouldn't hear of it. "That grave was made by ancient people and proves this place is suitable for habitation," he told her. Tamiko was convinced that the early deaths of her sons were due entirely to the curse of the grave and that the Miyaji family would eventually die out. She herself died in the spring of 1945 at the height of the American air campaign.

At the time of Tamiko's death, Miyaji's daughter Michiko was living in the house at Hake with her husband, Akiyama Tadao, who taught French at a private college in Tokyo. The Miyaji family was still influential when they married, but Akiyama had proposed to Michiko out of love, and he found it disagreeable to be looked upon as an adopted husband. Thus he was reluctant to move in with his father-in-law, even though he was urged to do so frequently after the air raids began. He finally agreed to escape to the house at Hake only after his own house in Shibuya burned down in May 1945.

Miyaji doted upon his daughter. Growing up with two brothers, Michiko had been a stubborn, feisty child, but she grew more demure when she reached the age when children become more aware of things. Her forehead jutted out a little and her jaw was broad, making her otherwise beautiful face resemble just a little the shape of a broad bean—in fact, her family nickname was Beany. She took pride in that nickname, and when her oldest brother was away at high school in Shikoku she always drew a picture of a broad bean in place of a signature in her letters to him.

Just as she was becoming more reserved, around the age of fourteen or fifteen, her nose became more prominent and distinguished and the Miss Broad Bean features disappeared. She had inherited her mother's white complexion, and she possessed a lovely face. She often received letters from the older students at her school and from middle school students in the neighborhood, but she never opened them. Instead, she handed them to her mother, who then had to go to the bother of complaining to the school about each one of them.

"It's all because you're careless," her mother would scold. Michiko would look surprised and stare at her—a reaction Tamiko found reassuring.

Michiko's childhood devotion to her oldest brother Shun'ichi, who was eight years her senior, took the place of any interest in boys. Shun'ichi resisted the pedantic cynicism of his father. Intoxicated at a young age with modern French literature, especially the works of Rimbaud, he led the wandering life of a young buck. He was tall, and his small, beautiful, oval face sat primly on his long neck. Everything he said was the Golden Rule to Michiko, and she asked his advice on every aspect of her life. She sent him all the money she received as gifts from various people at the midsummer festival of Obon and at New Year's.

As a result of his decadent lifestyle Shun'ichi contracted tuberculosis and died at the age of twenty-four. Following his death, Michiko transferred her adoration to her other brother, Keiji. Keiji had studied the piano ever since he was a little boy and wanted to be a composer. Michiko was forced to study with him and looked on with admiring eyes at how, in contrast to her own lack of progress, he could put together difficult compositions so effortlessly on the keyboard. Like Shun'ichi, Keiji also died of tuberculosis at the age of twenty-four. He had probably been infected by his older brother. It was strange that she alone showed no symptoms of the disease. "It's because of your jaw," her father explained to her, and she came to believe that this was definitely the reason, because Shun'ichi had once said of her, "Michiko's features are all beautiful. Only her jaw is a little wild."

Michiko was ardently pursued by Akiyama while she was still in school, and she married him when she was eighteen. She doted on Akiyama. However, when Keiji died three years after her marriage, she felt as though all the people she was devoted to would die and wondered if it was wrong to adore her husband so much. Interestingly, she began having these doubts at the same time she began to be troubled by Akiyama's habit of nibbling her ear whenever they made love.

She grew ever more beautiful. If you were to pick out any defects in her appearance, perhaps her torso was a bit too long—which was why her mother never allowed her to wear Western-style dresses if she could help it. Even when Michiko put on a kimono her mother grumbled that there was simply no way to tie the *obi* properly. Her father laughed and told Tamiko, "It's all right. In the Genroku period a long torso was a mark of beauty."

Around the time Michiko began to worry about Akiyama's habit of nibbling her ears, her father repeated his observation about Genroku beauties directly to her. He added a rather explicit joke about the bedroom charms of a woman with a long torso. He assumed his remarks were not inappropriate because his daughter was an adult, and so he was surprised when Michiko's large, unblinking eyes filled with tears as she stared at him.

Miyaji was a worldly man in some respects. He had, after all, been a regular customer at a small brothel in Yoshiwara during his student days in the Meiji period. Yet his thinking about sexual matters was really quite naive. He understood that a man has to respect a wife as the mistress of the household, but he invariably cheated on Tamiko when he was away on business trips. He did not consider his own behavior especially outrageous, and thus was incapable of seeing anything other than a woman's vanity in his daughter's tears. He could not fathom the subtle wound to Michiko's heart that lay behind her tears.

Just before this incident with her father, Michiko's so-called wifely duties had become painful for her. Akiyama was not licentious, but once he had grown accustomed to his wife's body he was no longer able to respond to Michiko's sentimentality except in a physical way. When a husband and wife are naively bound together, the manner of physical contact between them varies according to the proclivities of the man. The woman usually finds it difficult to humor him, and at this critical moment in a marriage, a man begins to cheat.

Akiyama was thirty when he married Michiko. It was a rather late marriage for him, and he had never slept with a woman until then. Born into a poor farming family in Saitama prefecture, he had thought about nothing but worldly success from the time he was a young boy. Quiet and timid by nature, he had no other option but to pursue the career of a scholar. He decided to study literature because he was not smart enough to distinguish himself in a rigorous discipline such as mathematics. French literature was just starting to gain popularity when he began his studies, and he chose Stendhal as his specialty because he empathized with Julien Sorel's ambition. A more important factor in his decision to study Stendhal was that other authors had been divvied up among the older students, and he was left with no choice but this slightly dated writer. His essays on Stendhal were published occasionally in specialist journals, but they were so filled with his close-minded passion and biases that they lacked the power to ever bring his star into fashion.

Akiyama was forced to accept with glum satisfaction his position as a teacher of French. Yet poring over Stendhal inspired in him an extremely feverish obsession with the practices of love and the taste for adultery of this author who cruised nineteenth-century salons. Although his experience as a teacher and his peaceful married life with Michiko bore no connection whatsoever with the adventures of that great egoist of the West, Akiyama yearned for the cynical techniques of love that Stendhal discussed in the treatise On Love and in various diaries and other writings.

Akiyama's peculiar yearnings played a role in the critical moment with Michiko alluded to above. Sheer cowardice had kept Akiyama from ever going to a prostitute. He was deathly afraid of venereal disease, which also explains why he had remained a virgin until he was thirty.

Keiji had disliked Akiyama. Michiko's parents were likewise unenthusiastic about the marriage, but Michiko had become utterly absorbed in the first candidate to come along. Akiyama was dark-skinned, skinny, and hopelessly nearsighted. Yet despite all that, Michiko somehow pictured him as a man to be doted upon. To a heart such as hers, with its propensity to adore others, an object of worship was a perennial necessity.

The cowardice of the husband and the patience of the wife allowed them to avert a crisis for a time. Then the hardships of war brought them closer together again. Because he was frail, Akiyama managed to avoid the military, but he was forced to serve instead as director of the student labor service, even during the summer breaks.

He would come home exhausted from continuous days of staff meetings. Michiko also wore herself out with fire training and bucket relays, and her heart seemed distracted. The constant pressure of living under the harsh conditions of wartime may have caused some couples to split up, but it strengthened the bonds between others.

No doubt moving in with Michiko's father was the main cause of the strains that reappeared in their relationship. The old man was seventy-five, and when the air raid sirens blared he would not run for shelter. "Whatever happens, I'll be here, so...," he would say, not budging from his desk. Akiyama had no choice but to reply, "All right, then, please excuse us," as he accompanied Michiko to the shelter. Akiyama frequently scolded her in the darkness, because she preferred to remain in the room with her father.

When rumors flew that Japan would surrender and that occupation forces would land at a nearby airfield, certain units of the army distributed potassium cyanide to anyone who wanted it. This poison became a topic for discussion in the Miyaji household. Akiyama had studied foreign literature, so he had faith that the American soldiers would behave properly, and he laughed off the delusions of the Japanese military. Michiko, however, told him that she would feel more comfortable having the poison, and her father, with his old-fashioned ways, supported her. This irritated Akiyama, who said to her, "If you want to get some, go ahead. But even if you decide to take it, just count me out." In the end he compromised by providing his wife with some sleeping pills he obtained from one of his colleagues, but the comment, "Just count me out," had wounded Michiko.

As the war drew to a close, Akiyama's family, who remained in their farming village in Saitama, helped out by sending food. Akiyama was pleased that for the first time he had been able to do something for the Miyaji family. Then came the unexpected postwar boom in publishing. The inexplicable popularity of the works of Stendhal was especially unexpected. The translations Akiyama had done years before were reprinted and distributed everywhere, and suddenly royalties started pouring in. The pension Michiko's father received was not enough to buy even a month's supply of rice for himself on the black market; and the stock certificates he owned were worse than scrap paper, they were actually a drain on his expenses. In contrast the share of money from Akiyama's earnings applied to the household budget increased, and he grew haughty as a result. He felt a vain pride that Michiko was ever more firmly tied to him. Somehow, as their lifestyle grew more comfortable, the ties of the heart that had connected them during the tribulations of the war were severed.

For all that, husbands and wives are strange creatures. Michiko no longer had any passion for her husband, but she continued to feel protective of him out of sheer force of habit. She had acquired that habit in reaction to the unfriendly attitude members of her family had displayed toward Akiyama when they were first married. And that feeling of protectiveness remained constant even after Akiyama had become the pillar that supported the Miyaji family. Her attitude irritated Akiyama.

The old man Miyaji was not easily discouraged. He sold his possessions. He sold the storehouse, which now held very little, and even some of his beloved trees. Each month he would without fail hand over to Michiko just enough money for her to supply what he needed to live. Moreover, he had the pine trees on the hill behind the house chopped down one by one to provide fuel to heat the water for their daily bath. He even had his own coffin made in advance from one large pine. Akiyama seemed strangely over-anxious about this matter, saying that because the wood of the coffin was nine millimeters thick, it would be heavy and difficult to deal with.

The person who bought the storehouse and trees was no stranger, but Miyaji's nephew, Ōno Eiji, who had moved a year earlier to a house on a plot of land separated from Chōsaku's place by a grove of chestnut trees.

Ōno was the child of Tamiko's younger sister, whose family, also former vassals of the Tokugawa lords, had moved to Shizuoka. In contrast to the Miyaji brothers, who mainly chose careers in the bureaucracy or the military, the Ōno's were a family of samurai who turned out to be surprisingly adept merchants. Eiji's father started work in the raw silk business in Yokohama. He had the flamboyant nature suited to the trade, but when the economic conditions of silk production changed in the last years of the Taishō period, he lost everything at once and retired to obscurity in his native village. He had three children at the time, the oldest being the nine-year-old Eiji. Eiji commuted back and forth from the Miyaji house to his middle school in Tokyo, and later, with the aid of a man who had once worked in his father's business, he graduated from the economics department of Keio University. In a bizarre coincidence, Eiji's benefactor had made a killing on stocks following the economic slump of 1919 that ruined Eiji's father. After graduating from Keio, Eiji went to work at a chemical factory owned by this same man. During the war the factory became a subcontractor for the military. Eiji's youthful recklessness was a perfect fit for the loose business practices of a wartime economy. He moved around setting up two or three subsidiaries in Manchuria and northern China, and then was placed in charge of a major plant near Fuchū. After the war he joined forces with a fish oil merchant and converted the factory to the production of soap.

Compared with the simple, old-fashioned life at Hake, everything about Ōno Eiji's house was flashy. He did not lay out his garden by planting a large number of trees, in the manner of the Miyaji house, but instead cut a terrace into the hillside and planted a flat lawn that extended all the way to the road. His house had originally been the second home of a stockbroker from Kayaba-chō. Ōno obtained the property at a bargain price because the owner, fearful of air raids even in the countryside, had moved further out to Ōme.

Eiji had spent part of his youth living in the same house with Michiko, but there had been no opportunity for the affections that come with youthful familiarity to sprout between them. To someone of Eiji's cheerful, carefree disposition, Michiko seemed a little gloomy. So it was no surprise that he ended up marrying Tomiko, who was in temperament the exact opposite of Michiko.

Tomiko was the daughter of a high-level executive who worked in a major corporation. She was born in Tokyo, but had moved from region to region with her father's postings. As a result, she had taken on the manners of several regions. Her cheerful flirtatiousness was in the Osaka style, while her prudence in managing her household was more in the style of Nagoya. The one constant was that at every girls' school she attended, she was the subject of gossip.

Ōno got to know Tomiko when she and a few of her bad companions, including several men, threw a wild party to celebrate her graduation from a special course at a women's school in Tokyo. This school did not have a very good reputation. Ōno, who was then a young company man with a taste for gaudy things, showed up at the invitation of a friend. He danced a lot, then took Tomiko to a separate room. All he got was a slap, but from then on he recklessly used every means of persuasion at his disposal, finally managing to get her and her parents to consent to their marriage.

Just when he thought everything was settled, Tomiko blurted out that she absolutely detested the prospect of a life together with Ōno and ran off to her older sister's house in Osaka. Ōno left work and chased after her. He was not permitted to meet her, but a week later Tomiko, who had returned to Tokyo, inexplicably agreed to marry him.

The circumstances behind this incident are a bit obscure. Tomiko's father believed that Ōno used some trick in Osaka to lure his daughter out and have sex with her. The older sister, however, knew that Tomiko had been carrying on an affair earlier, when she was in school in Osaka. Her lover was a married man.

Ōno and Tomiko's marriage ceremony was a splendid affair paid for by Ōno's former benefactor, who was now acting as guarantor. Ōno's father had died before the wedding, but his old mother came up to Tokyo from the countryside in Shizuoka for the first time in ages. She cried in front of everyone, but that had no effect on Ōno, who decided not to bring her to his new home.

Ōno dressed his wife up in all the luxuries he could afford. He invited his coworkers at the company to his house and enjoyed showing Tomiko off to them. He even permitted her a certain license in order to increase his sense of self-satisfaction. It gave him pleasure, for example, to let her kiss a younger employee, a former office boy, so that he might watch the youth turn bright red in embarrassment.

Ōno was tall and athletic. Tomiko was slight of build. Her face was proportionately small, her eyes and nose primly arranged. Her eyes, with their long lashes, were extremely large and set off by bow-shaped eyebrows. Ōno took pride in the fact that Tomiko's lips were thin and that she was skilled at kissing.

She exuded an air of joyful compliance with her husband's perverse preferences, but in front of her husband she would not let her flirtations go beyond the precise limits he permitted—except when she was drunk from sake. Under her husband's influence she became more capable of holding her liquor. Nonetheless, there were times, especially if Ōno got drunk before she did, when she aroused extremely dangerous desires in her husband's friends. For all that, she had never made a mistake, and it appeared that she treasured above all else her position as the free wife of a resourceful husband.

A year after they were married, Tomiko gave birth to a daughter. Ōno insisted that he still wanted a son, but Tomiko hated the idea. Somewhere along the way Ōno was conditioned to do as his wife said, and he had to agree to use the contraceptives that became her obsession. He was oblivious to the fact that she had come to regret having given birth to their child.

Tomiko still had a lover. She had continued her affair with the man she met in Osaka just before her wedding. This man, who had a wife and children, came to Tokyo on business now and then, and she would meet him at his hotel. Tomiko had never really loved any man, but she did love dangerous situations.

Keeping a mistress. Committing adultery. These are the natural consequences of monogamy. Such behaviors occur less frequently than many novels would lead you to believe, but they happen more often than society lets on. To put the matter another way, the extent to which cheating takes place equals the extent to which such behavior remains unknown to husbands or wives.

Tomiko managed to stay within permissible bounds with her husband's friends because she had this secret outlet. Her lover was eventually called up by the military and died in battle in the South Pacific. She was not especially broken up about his death.

It must be said that Tomiko loved Ōno in her own way. Men were creatures of no interest to her at all except as mirrors that reflected her own attractiveness. Since Ōno was the man who reacted most sensitively to her charms, she did not think ill of him.

Although Tomiko was now thirty, her small frame gave her the appearance of a woman of twenty-five. Every man who came to her house, even the men who made deliveries or who came by to take orders for goods, was dazzled by the mysterious charm radiating from her body. Chōsaku's second son, Kenji, would often volunteer to do odd jobs around her house, such as chopping firewood. Kenji, who had returned to his father's house at Hake after being repatriated from north China, confessed to his mother that he trembled every time he was near Tomiko's body. Similarly, the young man who delivered milk from the local farms every morning never just left the bottles at the kitchen entrance, but always made sure to call out "Madam!" and hand the milk directly to her.

Compared with the general level of postwar poverty, the Ōno house seemed all the more prosperous. They stocked up on large quantities of black-market goods, and Ōno was able to offer his guests a luxurious menu of foods that he obtained surreptitiously. Tomiko was skilled at preparing Chinese cuisine, and Ōno entertained many of his business guests at home. Michiko's father always sneered at Ōno's lifestyle, but when he had to move his garden trees to Ōno's place, he stopped criticizing him.

"He's a real man in his own fashion," the elder Miyaji would say. "No one else could keep that wife of his." And indeed Tomiko's family, especially the older sister in Osaka, was deeply grateful to Ōno. For his part, Ōno was faithful to Tomiko in name only. He secretly carried on numerous affairs with the women who worked at his company.

Akiyama took it badly that someone appeared in the neighborhood who could compete with the newfound success of his translations. At first he joined Michiko's father in bad-mouthing Ōno, but then for some reason he abruptly stopped the criticism. Not only that, he started killing time in the evenings by going on what he called a stroll—walking along the road at the bottom of the hillside for a block or so and then dropping by the Ōno house. Miyaji knew his son-in-law all too well and saw this ruse for what it was. Akiyama had become attracted to Tomiko. Miyaji despised Akiyama's masculine charms, but he was not in the least bit worried because he was fully aware of Tomiko's self-centeredness.

The old man claimed he would live a long time and keep watch on the revival of Japan, which had finally returned to a proper course as a result of the defeat. However, he died suddenly of a heart attack near the end of 1946.

Michiko wept inconsolably. She realized once more just how much she had relied on her father. At the same time, she came to realize just how little she could depend upon her husband. There was no one else she could count on among her relatives, who were scattered here and there. Ōno was in love with his business and his wife. Her uncle Tōgo had killed himself, and the only surviving members of his family were his second wife, who did not come from a particularly distinguished background, and her small child. Michiko had never visited them while her uncle was alive. That left only Tsutomu, a college student who was Tōgo's son from a previous marriage, which had ended in divorce. Tsutomu had often visited the house at Hake in earlier years. He had been called up in the student draft of 1943 and sent off to Burma. She had had no news of him since.

She felt all alone. She was no longer confident that she could continue to bear her isolation as she had previously. The atmosphere surrounding a death frequently causes people to imagine the worst. Still, the fact remained that her life up to then had been lived entirely in the shadow of her father.

Tomiko cried and comforted Michiko. There was some goodness in her flirtatious heart.

The funeral was a simple affair. It had been so long since his retirement from the bureaucracy that only a few people connected with the railroads attended. Their place was occupied by a crowd of people from Ōno's company. The neighbors made up by far the largest group of mourners. It had been fifteen years since Miyaji moved permanently to this region; and while his sarcasm and pedantry made him seem difficult to approach, if you mentioned "Mr. Miyaji of Hake," everyone in the neighborhood, from farmers to rickshaw men, knew who you meant. His ashes were interred alongside those of his wife and sons in the family grave in Tama Cemetery, which was across from Hake on the opposite bank of the Nogawa.

With the funeral and the commotion attending it finally out of the way, Michiko's married life returned to its former tranquility. Akiyama spent some money on major repairs to the dilapidated house. He invited his friends, who had gradually increased in number, to what amounted to an open house for the renovated home. He did not realize that all of this was an affront to Michiko.

This was the state of the residents of Hake in June of the third year following the end of the war, which is the time this story begins. Akiyama was forty-one, Michiko was twenty-nine, Ōno was forty, Tomiko was thirty, and her daughter Yukiko was nine.

Whenever people from the city, weary with concerns about money and food, visited these two houses, they went home either amazed or dejected that such a relaxed realm could exist in this harsh world. The houses commanded a view from the hillside of the greening Tama basin. Looking out at the clustered groves, in which a pale green seemed to be permanently fixed, people wondered if even the trees at Hake preserved the new colors of spring. Hearing that the pale green was chestnut blossoms, they felt even more amazed or dejected. Chestnuts were a profitable crop for the farmers of this area, so close to the city, and groves thickly covered the ground wherever you looked.

A new resident would soon arrive in Hake—Miyaji's nephew, Tsutomu, who had not yet returned from Burma at the time of the old man's death. The behavior of this young man of twenty-four following his repatriation brought considerable grief to the people of Hake, especially its women. But all of that can be told in conjunction with his entrance to the story.

CHAPTER 2

AN EX-SOLDIER

An incident took place at Hake at just about the time this story begins. Strictly speaking, it did not actually take place at Hake, but was closely related to the people there. Chōsaku's second son Kenji broke into a house beyond the rail line and was killed by the owner.

It happened at ten o'clock on a May evening. The owner, a former army officer, had gone out, and when he returned he found Kenji threatening his wife with the kind of knife used to slice sashimi. The man pulled a pistol from the closet and shot at Kenji. The bullet missed, but Kenji was stabbed in the back with the sashimi knife as he tried to scramble out the window to escape. He died in hospital ten hours later. The former officer was charged with using excessive force in self-defense and with illegal possession of a firearm.

The owner claimed the pistol was merely for intimidation and that he had fired at the feet of the intruder. But when Kenji, in a panic, threw the knife at the man's chest, the owner had been overcome by the urge to kill. Kenji died without saying anything, leaving many details about the incident unsettled. Since he was carrying no money on him, it wasn't clear if he had broken in with the intent to rob. According to some, he was going there to have an affair with the wife. She was a fair-skinned beauty who liked to stand nonchalantly by the gate in the evenings.

Kenji had worn a mask. One young man with a literary bent remarked that he had read a story about a character who donned a mask in order to procure a prostitute who was a relative. This young man came to the shrewd conclusion that Kenji was just pretending to be a burglar so that he could rape a woman he had fallen for.

Kenji's mother, Ohama, rejected all explanations based on burglary or sexual desire. Even so, Kenji had had a number of indiscriminate affairs with women in the area following his demobilization. Recently, more and more streetwalkers had been seen in the neighborhood, and his friends eventually let slip that he had been seeing one of them, and that he had been strapped for money. In the end the incident was left unresolved. The only things known for sure were that Kenji was dead, and that the pistol hidden away by the owner of the house had been discovered.

Ohama frequently visited Tomiko's house to complain about her son's death.

"Such an outrageous thing ought never to happen, let alone to such a quiet boy." As Ohama told it, "The sashimi knife actually belonged to the couple, which means that whore conspired with her husband to kill my son."

It was a little odd that Ohama should so persistently come to tell Tomiko about her son.

"And you treated him with such great kindness as well," Ohama said, blubbering all over again. This was too much for Tomiko. There was no denying that on occasion she had spoken amiably with him in gratitude for his help in procuring black-market rice or splitting firewood. But that was all there was to it—though she knew very well how Kenji would interpret her friendliness.

Ohama, like all mothers, was sensitive to her son's feelings toward the opposite sex. Her sensitivity was the consequence of the way in which she, as a wife and mother, suppressed such emotions.

One day Tomiko went to talk with Michiko about the incident. Michiko was terribly ignorant of the world, and Tomiko thought she was doing a kindness by keeping Michiko up to date on the latest gossip. Of course Tomiko also secretly desired to boast about Kenji's special admiration for her.

The afternoon sky was clear. Akiyama was away. Michiko was sitting alone on the veranda mending her husband's summer clothes. Whenever Tomiko arrived at Michiko's place, she invariably felt a slight sense of superiority. In addition to her material sense of superiority—her possessions were new compared to Michiko's, after all—her experience with her lover made her feel that Michiko was a fool to continue obeying a tedious, unaccomplished man like Akiyama. Tomiko would never even touch her husband's kimono.

Tomiko chattered away while Michiko listened and continued her sewing. Tomiko's memory was strong, and she was good at telling stories.

The possibility that sexual desire might have been Kenji's motive seemed to be news to Michiko. She murmured a few disinterested "Hmmm's" and "That's terrible's" as she worked, but when Tomiko's story reached the point about his passions, Michiko suddenly lifted her head.

Her expression was serious. Tomiko had long thought Michiko a hypocrite, so she could not help noting this sudden reaction. Tomiko was in the habit of conjecturing about other people from her own experience, so she concluded that Kenji had displayed a certain interest, which Michiko in turn had found hard to ignore. Tomiko thus gave an exaggerated account of Ohama's conspiracy theory.

Michiko once more lowered her eyes and slowly spread the sewing in front of her. She again displayed her earlier indifference, and Tomiko gave up.

As it turns out, Tomiko's conjecture was partly correct, partly mistaken. Michiko had known Kenji since childhood. He was four years younger, but had been the neighborhood bully in elementary school. He had also been popular with the girl students. Michiko had been terribly bullied by him. Of course, when Michiko went off to school, then married and moved to Tokyo, their relationship, like all childhood friendships, grew more distant than the relationship of travelers who casually meet on the way. They became acquainted again only because Michiko's house had been firebombed and she had to return to Hake, and Kenji had been demobilized the year after the war ended.

Michiko was shocked that along the way he had become a typical young man of the town—his thick neck sinking into his shoulders, his stocky build, his thick lips pursed together as though he was enduring something. These features all made a woman like her feel disgust. Whenever she passed by the front of Chōsaku's house on the way to Ōno's place on some errand, Kenji, working a field in the distance, would stop his hoeing and stare after her. For some reason his attitude really bothered her.

One morning she had been working on the veranda when she lifted her head and saw Kenji standing there. His clothes, the kind issued to demobbed soldiers, were dirty, and he said something mundane like, "Need any potatoes?" She would recall that scene from time to time, wondering why it was that, when she first caught sight of him standing there, she had not scolded him for approaching so stealthily.

Her anger, however, was not the sole reason she remembered that moment. For the Kenji she had seen just then bore a striking resemblance to her cousin Tsutomu when he first arrived at her house after returning from Burma.

On a warm February morning, not long after her father had died, she was on the veranda as usual when suddenly Tsutomu appeared in his ex-soldier's clothing, standing near the edge of the garden. Her first reaction was unpleasant, since she thought that it was Kenji who had dropped by. But as soon as she recognized Tsutomu, she thought she was seeing a ghost. He laughed and moved closer, saying, "I'm no ghost! See, I've got legs!" She remembered that even though it was February, his complexion was dark, like that of a person who had gone skiing.

Tsutomu was the son of the first wife of Michiko's uncle, Tōgo, who had committed suicide. Tsutomu's flamboyant mother had been born into a distinguished military family, but she was not up to the sobriety and prudence of his father. Eventually she fled, leaving her son behind. When his father remarried, Tsutomu became a superfluous member of the family and was sent off at an early age to a boarding house to attend private school. Unlike most other students taken in the draft, he seemed rather happy to leave.

There had been no communication from him after he was drafted until the day when, out of the blue, he came ambling back, having survived his experience as a POW. He disembarked at Uraga, but went straight through Nakano, where his family's house was, and proceeded immediately to Hake. He said he decided to come to Hake because he figured the house in Nakano had burned down. But it was more likely that, having been sent away as a child, he no longer considered the Nakano residence his home.

Michiko told him his family house was still standing, and, after serving him lunch, sent him on his way. She was a little shocked when he showed no reaction to the news of his father's suicide.

Tsutomu's stepmother was upset. With the return of Tsutomu the inheritance of the estate, consisting mainly of the Nakano house that had survived the fire bombings, was to be executed under the old civil code just before reforms in the law were enacted. Michiko and the others assumed that the largest part of the estate would go to the stepmother and her child in accordance with emergency measures that were to take effect on May 3; but their expectations were betrayed, and Tsutomu gave only half the estate to his stepmother.

Once he got his hands on some of the money from the disposal of the house and property, he began to live the willful life of a student. He ignored the advice of Michiko to come and stay at Hake, opting instead to live at the house of a former school friend. He hardly ever visited Hake.

Tsutomu was enrolled, coincidentally, at the same private college where Akiyama taught. The stories Akiyama told Michiko about Tsutomu's lifestyle caused her a great deal of anxiety. It wasn't just that he rarely attended classes, but that he seemed to enjoy surrendering himself to the atmosphere of dissolution and irresponsibility that had engulfed young men and women after the war.

The Tsutomu Michiko had once known was a quiet, lonely young man. The sharp change in his character that occurred after he went to the army troubled her heart every time she saw an article in the newspaper describing the degenerate behavior of former soldiers of the Special Attack Forces. He was bound to run through his small inheritance quickly.

She had been agitated by the story of Kenji's burglary and the sexual desire that had driven him because she felt a fleeting fear in her heart that Tsutomu might do something similar. Moreover, her apprehension was further compounded when Tomiko said to her, "Don't you think Kenji resembles Tsutomu in some ways." Tomiko's statement confirmed Michiko's impression of Tsutomu, and at the same time aroused the fear in Michiko that Tomiko was coming on to Tsutomu in the same way she did to all the young men in the neighborhood. Once, on one of Tsutomu's rare visits to Hake, Tomiko's flirting and Tsutomu's casual reaction had not escaped her attention.

The character who had become such an object of concern for these two women was at that very moment gradually approaching Hake, strolling along the level ground on the crest of the slope.

A plane was soaring through the clear June sky. As an ex-soldier, Tsutomu found it hard to accept that he need not be on his guard against a plane's voluptuous silver body and its clear, keening roar.

He was wearing the government-surplus airman's uniform he had obtained after he had been demobilized. There were lots of zippers on the sleeves and hems, and the pockets of his trousers stretched down to the front of his kneecaps. The outfit made him stick out in a crowd and had a double meaning for him. First, he liked being identified by others as a veteran. This identification was useful for concealing ideas he nurtured secretly inside, for he believed that no one would understand if he spoke them aloud. Second, he knew that he had acquired those ideas at the front—that they were the ideas of an ex-soldier. Thus he felt pride at being identified as a veteran, and he wanted to show off.

The chaos of defeat only strengthened the conviction he had long nurtured deep inside as a stepchild that the only person he could rely on was himself. In addition, the degradation of being a POW had caused him to lose all faith in humanity. The behavior of adults in a defeated Japan, which he had witnessed after demobilization, merely confirmed his conviction. He had no interest in the student movement, and he did not believe in democracy.

To report that his initial response to the news of his father's death was a sense of liberation might make him seem inhuman. Yet that is how he really felt. He had seen so many die at the front, and he knew just how much trouble death could save. He loved his father, but he felt nothing special about his passing. The dead were gone. That was all there was to it. He himself might have been dead and gone.

Michiko's father had mocked the sentimental patriotism that was the apparent motive behind his younger brother's suicide. But the elder Miyaji could see that Tōgo, ruined by the defeat, had also killed himself out of despair at a future in which he would have to bear the burden of a selfish wife and a small child. Tsutomu was of much the same mind. He felt no deep emotion over his father's death, but rather saw the advantage of severing the one connection that tied him to his stepmother and her child.

Had Tsutomu's views on life and death been influenced by his childhood exposure to the military character of his father? This was a difficult question to resolve, because in the present age the social position of "soldier" had disappeared.

Tsutomu's egotism was apparent in the way he refused to give up any of the privileges he held as the last presumed heir to his father's estate under the old civil code. One of the lessons he had learned at the front was that you must use without delay any rights that fall to you by chance. As a result of that lesson, he intended to live selfishly for as long as the small estate held out. When his inheritance was exhausted, he intended to act according to the battlefield principle that you deal with things when the time comes and circumstances warrant.

Despite the fact that he was nothing more than a lazy idler, he intended to live life to the utmost. He was not particularly adept at thinking deeply about things. Once in a while, whenever he was absorbed in some serious thought, he would go for a walk. Suddenly he would be caught up in the illusion that the green fields of Burma had sprung open around him. The center of these fields was always the spot on the ground before him where he fixed his eyes. Cannons would roar and people would groan. Afraid that his hallucination would turn into reality, he could not look up. Although he would eventually come to his senses and realize that he was simply on a street corner in a large city in Japan, the hallucination inevitably disrupted his thoughts.

He had lost his virginity at the front. Near the end of the war, when the army was cut off in the mountains of southern Tongu, there was a nurse who had no choice but to have sex with the soldiers if she wanted to survive. His youthful lust and curiosity got the best of him, but he could never forget the smell of the hair of a woman who had cast away all shame for the sake of food.

Following his repatriation, he gave himself over to affairs with degenerate students. The sweaty hair of those ugly women was pleasurable to him because it brought back the bizarre sensation he had experienced in that thatched hut in the mountains of Burma. His good looks and his cruelty gave him many opportunities for success.

He did not visit Hake very often because he had a degree of respect for his cousin. He felt inclined to visit her today after a long absence because he had grown weary of his way of life. Even he had some small expectations.

Hurrying past the prostitutes and their tricks crowding near the station, he passed through an empty alley. The old Musashino road came into sight. Black soil ran in uniform rows between the low, dry-paddy rice plants. The color of that soil was the only thing that had stirred any nostalgia in him after his return from the tropics. He had lost hope in humanity, but he loved nature. Soldiering is a profession where one is frequently in contact with nature.

He moved along some tea hedges and walked through a chestnut grove. Just as he was tiring of the road, which ran on for some distance through dry-cultivated fields, he arrived at a spot where the tall trees covering the slope of Hake came into view.

That stand of trees had been a familiar sight to him since childhood. Oak, cedar, zelkova—the sight of the trees decorating the background of Miyaji's land was the most nostalgic image of his lonely youth. He remembered that just coming here had been a pleasure in those days.

The elder Miyaji's land straddled the lane that wound from the lower road at Hake along the upper slope of the hillside. Unlike the other houses there, the Miyaji residence did not have a gate facing this upper lane, which was closer to the station. This was in keeping with the old man's odd, pedantic nature. He once said, "This area was originally developed from the direction of the Tamagawa, which is to the south. The temples and shrines all face Fuchū. That is in accord with nature." Only a small wooden door opened onto the upper lane, and Michiko's father would not permit any visitor, not even Tsutomu, to enter from that door.

When that weather-beaten wooden door came into view, Tsutomu instantly felt the urge to enter. The door was latched, but he was able to undo it easily by sticking his hand through the hedgerow on the side. Pushing the wooden door open, he felt a mysterious joy. He thought it was simply the joy of a childish prank, but this kind of secretive behavior was also a habit he had acquired at the front, where he had been forced always to make surprise attacks. He had grown fond of making surprise attacks.

He passed through the wooden door and came out onto a level space of about 110 square meters. Michiko's father had originally planned the space with the intention of building a house there for his oldest son. Now it was allowed to grow wild, and yellow rose, vigorously cultivated in this region, was blooming lushly over the ground amidst the cedar and zelkova, hiding the grasses beneath.

Though he had come to Hake many times, he had hardly ever set foot in this place. His interest in the topography of unfamiliar landscapes was another soldierly habit he had acquired. Defeated soldiers are always watching for avenues of escape when they are on the march.

He examined the path. It was overgrown by grass as it wound away from the wooden door. The slope to the right was visible all the way to a spot where someone had fashioned steps from tree branches. The path then undulated down until it came to the edge of the veranda. The unfamiliar shape of the back roof seemed strangely severe, blocking the space below as though holding up the slope.

A path to nowhere, a feature found in all gardens, split off faintly to the left. It led to top of the cliff where the spring at Hake was concealed.

The edge of the property was overgrown with thick-stemmed bamboo that had crept over from Chōsaku's land next door. Looking at the small hollow surrounded by the yellow rose, Tsutomu recalled how he would hide there with Michiko whenever they played hide-and-seek long ago. The feeling of being a conspirator, the memories of Michiko's warm body and the smell of her young hair—all of this came back to him. As he crouched in the hollow, the murmuring of the stream grew louder. He could see the figures of two women below on the veranda, which was fronted by a pond created by damming the stream.

Michiko sat inside the veranda. Tomiko was seated at the edge. Michiko was sewing with her back half turned to him. Though he was over sixty feet away, Tsutomu, with a sentry's gaze, was able to distinguish the shape of her ears, familiar to him from childhood.

This was the first time in his life that he had been able to watch her in a leisurely manner. He thought it a very strange state of affairs. "State of affairs"—the vocabulary of an ex-soldier.

Watching her from behind, he saw that she had not changed a bit from the time she was a bride. *When I first came back here after the war,* he thought, *she made a really odd face. But her expression changed right away and she looked overjoyed. No one else was that happy for me when I got back. Come to think of it, she was the only one who cried for me when I went off to the army. I was stupid not to have stayed in touch. She's probably been lonely since my uncle died. She's as lonely as I am.*

Hold on now. There's still Akiyama. What a nasty bastard. He and Stendhal make a weird combination. I haven't read Stendhal, so I don't know much about him. But my friend in the French department says Akiyama's lectures take Stendhal by the feet and drag him down to his level.

It was fortunate for Akiyama that Tsutomu had not read of the intermarriage in *The Charterhouse of Parma.* If he had, he might have been inclined to give a different name to the emotions he was feeling toward his cousin at this moment.

Tsutomu looked over at Tomiko. She was almost directly in front of him. *Is a woman like that really beautiful? When she first looked at me, her eyes seemed to say she was willing, and I thought there was some affection there. But I bet she looks at everybody that way. Being loved by a woman like her is no big deal. She's skinny. And I wonder if she's aware of those fine wrinkles starting to crease her face? Those are the kind that will spread surprisingly fast.*

In Tomiko's defense, it must be said that Tsutomu was looking at her with a critical eye because he felt favorably disposed toward Michiko.

If he could have heard from where he was crouching what Tomiko was saying just then, he would have been grateful to her.

The conversation between these two women was broken off earlier in order to discuss Tsutomu's background. All the while they had been talking about the connection between his behavior and the crime committed by Chōsaku's son, Kenji. Concluding her thoughts on the matter, Tomiko made the following proposal.

"Shall I have Tsutomu come over to my house?" she said. "Yukiko now has to take English classes at her school, and we're worried about it. If he helps us out and we supervise him, things may improve a bit. "

Michiko was annoyed by Tomiko's presumptuousness. After all, she was Tsutomu's cousin, not Tomiko.

Just then Tomiko glanced up toward the thicket where Tsutomu was hiding. He tried rustling the yellow rose plants a little, but when he saw the fear in Tomiko's face he stood up, revealing his torso. He waved to her and Tomiko also stood up.

Tomiko's sudden movement startled Michiko. As she turned in the direction Tomiko was looking, she couldn't help noticing the blush spreading quickly over Tomiko's face. Michiko could not easily fathom the meaning of this reaction, but in any case she had never seen her cousin's coquettish wife wear such an expression. Later she would contemplate why she thought the expression so ugly at the time.

"Tsutomu!" Tomiko cried out.

Tsutomu laughed and with great strides came down a path bordered by the branches of the trees. He saw that Michiko, who had glanced at him, had already turned her face away.

The ex-soldier sat down on the veranda and talked cheerfully, just like any twenty-four-year-old sitting between two beautiful women. However, he noticed that Michiko's eyes never met his. Even when he pointed out their old mutual hiding place on top of the cliff, he had no effect on her. He wondered if, out of her sense of filial duty, she was angry with him because he had entered through the wooden door at the rear, breaking his uncle's prohibition.

Chapter 3

The Conditions for Adultery

Michiko's father had slightly underestimated his son-in-law. The old man despised Akiyama and dismissed his unusual interest in Tomiko as nothing more than a whim. But there was nothing capricious in the old peasant blood that flowed through the veins of this French teacher. Akiyama, who at first glance seemed so reserved, fully intended to seduce Tomiko. Michiko had also taken note of her husband's frequent strolls over to Tomiko's house, but she tended to follow her father in everything and so made nothing more of it.

Beyond that, when she considered the habits they had developed during their years of marriage, Michiko did not think her husband could possibly do anything that might have serious consequences.

Akiyama's desire for Tomiko was stimulated directly by her flirtatiousness, but the deeper reason for his interest in her was his dissatisfaction with Michiko's body. He had not gone to a prostitute because he was basically stingy and had a pathological fear of venereal disease. In these respects a married woman like Tomiko was safe. Moreover, she met another of his conditions: she would not cost a lot of money. In the end, such calculations would never have occurred to the good-natured Michiko and her father.

Contrary to expectation, this kind of self-interest is the basis of the conditions for adultery. It goes without saying that a kind of immorality on the part of the couple involved is also needed. There was never much room for morals in the academic Akiyama's belief in worldly success. His interest in adultery was for the most part cultivated by his close study of the works of Stendhal. The great amorist of the nineteenth-century salons certainly did not consider the relationship between husband and wife a major obstacle to an affair. Rather, marriage was a pleasurable obstacle that aroused passion and led to greatness. Akiyama, a fantasist who had never known love, took that passion quite seriously—that is to say, selfishly—without ever considering the differences in epochs or national temperaments.

At that time a law repealing the old statute criminalizing adultery had passed through the appropriate legislative committees and was set to take effect at the end of the year. To be sure, this change in the law spurred on Akiyama's hopes. No doubt the intentions of progressive intellectuals, who sought to undo feudal penalties that dealt harshly only with wives, were well meaning. But the practical effect of the repeal of the old statute was merely to lessen the responsibility of male adulterers. It did not increase the freedom of wives, who remained economically dependent on men. At the very least, the psychological impact of the measure, which abolished existing law, was to embolden men. Akiyama for one no longer needed to fear prison clothes and a wattle hat.

The coquettishness Tomiko showed Akiyama was no more than she showed all men. Akiyama, a student of French literature, understood that well enough. His academic background, however, was of no real use in helping him understand Tomiko's bewildering behavior. Naturally men do not comprehend every nuance of a woman's flirting; and when all is said and done men who are in love have no other guide but their own passion. Still, insofar as he thought he simply wanted to seduce her, Akiyama's feelings remained lukewarm. And because he felt that way, he was even more compelled to try grasping fully the meaning of every nuance of Tomiko's coquetry.

Like all potential lovers who are already married, Akiyama and Tomiko began by talking about their dissatisfaction with their spouses. She alluded to Ōno's lack of understanding. He lamented Michiko's coldness. Their complaints, however, had slightly different meanings.

Ōno and Michiko were cousins, which is to say, they were the heirs to Hake. Thus, for Akiyama and Tomiko, outsiders related only by marriage, there was a familial dimension in their expressions of dissatisfaction.

Because of the feudal customs constraining women, Tomiko understood the significance of family ties. Akiyama on the other hand, dazzled by his own fantasies, did not. He grew restless listening to Tomiko prattle endlessly about minute household details whenever she complained about Ōno as a husband.

Akiyama had no confidence in his own manhood, but he was not far off the mark when he decided to woo Tomiko by discussing literature. Tomiko was sick of all the talk about money and commodities she heard from the brokers and salaried workers who were her husband's associates. Akiyama's conversations were fresh to her.

One evening in May the repeal of the adultery statute came up repeatedly in their conversation. They were out on the terrace of Tomiko's house, which commanded a view of the Tama basin and of Mt. Fuji. Talking until Ōno came home from his factory nearby, there was the merest whisper of danger in their conversation, for it was beyond their power to make much headway on the problem. A magazine commentator had made the persuasive argument that the repeal of a punishment does not necessarily sweep away ethical control. Akiyama knew that it was not to his advantage to weave into a conversation about adulterous love the utilitarian motive that one would not be punished.

Akiyama attempted to prove that monogamy was irrational and that adultery was not at all evil when examined in light of innate human nature. Though this idea may sound exceedingly peculiar, Akiyama cited Friedrich Engels's *The Origins of the Family, Private Property, and the State* in support of his position.

The fundamental idea of this classical work of Communism is that the accumulation of capital breaks up familial communities and creates a national form of control. The idea that the system of monogamy arose with private property is simply a general concept presented to reinforce the work's fundamental claims. Akiyama had first encountered this work after he had turned forty and had come to regard nation and society with the smug mindset of a petit bourgeois egoist. As a result, he responded only to the secondary idea, which just now provided him a convenient justification for rejecting both his own and Tomiko's married lives.

Tomiko listened with apparent interest to Akiyama's argument as he droned on about the rationality of ancient blood kinship and of marriages decided by couples on their own. From the beginning Tomiko had loved her husband only as a source of income. Since she had once had a lover, she knew all about Akiyama's ideas from personal experience. Her smile never left her face as they chatted, which he took as a sign of her agreement. He was therefore surprised, when he finished speaking, to find that she disagreed with him.

"All that stuff's in the distant past," she said. "Civilization has progressed, and without monogamy women would have no one to rely on."

Her manner of speech merely reflected the habit of a coquette who teases a man by contradicting him. But Akiyama, as always, took her remark seriously, and later regretted that he had been unable to challenge it at the time.

On the day Tsutomu visited Hake for the first time in several months, Tomiko also just happened to have dropped by. She had come over to gossip about the incident involving Ogino Kenji, but there was another reason for her visit. She and Ōno were hosting a party that evening for a Communist party official named Kaizuka. Kaizuka had once worked at Ōno's company, and after he quit he took up a position as secretary for a labor union. Ōno thought Akiyama's intellectual conversation could enliven the dinner, so he told Tomiko to invite him.

When Akiyama got home from the college at around four o'clock, Tomiko remembered why she had dropped by, and extended the invitation.

"He says you'll get the inside story on current affairs," she said. "This is perfect timing. Tsutomu, you should come too."

Akiyama did not care for Tsutomu. In his eyes Tsutomu resembled one of Stendhal's young heroes just a bit too closely.

It was certainly the case that Tsutomu possessed a noble-looking face and youthful grace, but he did not really resemble Julien or Fabrizio all that much. He had known nothing but the misfortune of a stepchild, and so lacked the energy that distinguished those two. The only thing he shared in common with these manly characters was youthfulness. If Akiyama had thought it over carefully, he would have realized that he always felt an antipathy towards almost every young man. Perhaps he was more aware of his special dislike towards Tsutomu because his wife was Tsutomu's cousin.

Akiyama was not at all pleased to have to accompany Tsutomu that evening, but at least having a Communist party member there would give him an opening to discuss Engels in front of Tomiko. According to Akiyama's interpretation, Engels argued that the system of monogamous marriage would be maintained through the free will of men and women in the ideal communist society of the future. Akiyama figured that he could steer the discussion in a convenient direction by contrasting what Engels wrote with the sexual license of the Soviet Union, about which he knew a smattering.

Tomiko had extended the invitation to Michiko, but Akiyama put a stop to it. He told Michiko, "That's no place for you."

Dinner began at seven o'clock in the family room facing the lawn. Ōno loved having guests. He took particular pride in avoiding the formal Japanese-style room and bringing his guests into the family room. After the war it was a fairly common custom to provide an abundance of good foods in lieu of a formal setting. Ōno changed into a light summer robe. Sitting cross-legged at the seat of honor, he began to drink heavily in front of his three guests, who were not drinking. He was soon drunk and started to tease his guest of honor, the Communist official Kaizuka. He kept saying, "No matter how you slice it, poverty is no good. Nothing comes of poverty."

Kaizuka was a reserved man in his thirties. With Ōno's help he had found a haven during the war by joining the chemical company.

Ōno had hired Kaizuka even though he knew his personal history. Ōno was no fellow traveler, however, for he was constitutionally indifferent to politics. Kaizuka performed his work with precision and got along with his fellow workers. Setting aside his beliefs, he really was a pretty normal fellow.

Ōno did not invite Kaizuka to dinner that day merely for the purpose of hearing about the underside of politics only a minority party knows. And for his part, Kaizuka had come with the purpose of increasing support for his party among the acquaintances of his former guarantor. All of this was taking place shortly after the failure of the February 1 strike, when the Party had to retreat and shift to a strategy of rallying the intellectuals.

The conversation began casually with some reminiscences, but it soon took on a political tone. When it did, Kaizuka, who had been rather quiet, suddenly found his voice. He pointed out the impact of the failure of the February 1 strike on the national consciousness of the people. Given the way he chattered on as though he were making a speech, it was apparent that he had given talks on this topic at a number of places.

Tsutomu, the ex-soldier, had no interest in politics. He had a vague sense that it was dangerous to advocate nationalism, which ran counter to the trend of the time. But from the viewpoint of military strategy, politics provided no possibility of decisive victory and would always be hopelessly compromised by reacting to immediate circumstances. He did not join in the conversation.

Akiyama, who likewise had no interest in politics, felt the same as Tsutomu. Nonetheless, he jumped right into the discussion.

"Won't strengthening national consciousness promote a return of fascist elements?" he asked.

"Perhaps," said Kaizuka. "But now there are legal restraints on such people, so it's unlikely that many fascists will resurface."

"You've always been an optimist, Kaizuka." Ōno laughed and glanced over at Tomiko, who was sitting off to the side.

After their maid, Kaneya, took Yukiko to her room and put her to bed, Tomiko was kept busy running back and forth to the kitchen by herself. She finally finished bringing in the food and sat down.

To illustrate Kaizuka's optimism, Ōno and Tomiko together told a story from the days when he worked for them. Kaizuka evidently fell in love with a college student who was extremely intelligent. He had brushed aside Ōno's opposition to his plan to marry the woman, but, because she was virulently anti-Communist, Kaizuka was suffering. Ōno told him that an intellectual wife was trouble and that he should give up on her. Kaizuka, however, vowed that he would somehow find a way to win her over. Ōno mocked Kaizuka's confidence, saying that it reflected an optimism that ignored the fundamental realities of the life of a married couple, and that Kaizuka was violating a central tenet of his party, the ideal of equal rights for men and women.

The instant Ōno uttered the words "equal rights for men and women," Akiyama seized his chance to bring up the topic of the recent repeal of the adultery law. Ōno agreed with the repeal.

"No husband," he said, "has ever sued for divorce solely on the grounds that he was shamed because some guy cheated on him with his wife. Even when people do file a complaint, the matter is usually settled privately. So what's the big controversy about getting rid of such a law?"

"The issue is whether to abolish the crime for both men and women," Akiyama replied, "or to punish both men and women."

A subtle expression flitted over Ōno's face. If both men and women were punished, then he would be forced to keep his hands off his female workers. He fell silent.

"Is adultery a crime in the Soviet Union?" Akiyama put the question to Kaizuka.

"No, it isn't."

"And is there adultery there?"

"I don't know. I imagine it goes on."

"According to *The Origin of the Family, Private Property, and the State*," Akiyama said, "Engels claims that monogamy will likely continue in the communist society of the future. But I think that claim contradicts the concept of sexual love he included in his historical account of mixed and group marriages in primitive societies. What do you think? I get the impression that Engels distorted his analysis so as not to upset the familial sensibilities of the German petit bourgeois of his day."

This was an agile, Stendhalian observation. But its basic premise was wrong, since Engels argued that one could make only passive predictions about the future. For his part, Kaizuka did not remember much about this classic.

"Perhaps Engels had such ideas," he said. "So what?"

"I don't know much about the sex lives of present-day Soviet men and women," said Akiyama, "but doesn't it contradict Engels's prediction?"

"Not at all. Sometimes during a revolutionary period there may be sexual license, but right now the Soviet Union is being ridiculed by bourgeois critics for its support of families. If you get a divorce in the Soviet Union, ten per cent of your income, which is based on your work quota, is taken as a maintenance payment. So the number of divorces an individual can afford over a lifetime is limited."

The discussion was not going at all in the direction Akiyama had hoped.

"Perhaps that's because there's still a disparity between the incomes of men and women," he insisted. "If the ideal communist society of the future is achieved, such differences will disappear. What do you think will happen then?"

Kaizuka found Akiyama's persistence unsettling.

"I haven't the faintest idea. We're in a transitional age, and there are a lot more important things to consider than that."

But Akiyama would not feel satisfied until he had spit out everything he had gleaned from Engels.

"In any case," he said, "if the descriptions of primitive society in Engels's account are accurate, then monogamy is irrational. In ancient times it was nearly impossible for a woman to marry only one man. Evidently she would be forced, as a penalty, to have sex with a number of men before marriage."

"Well, now, that's an encouraging report" Ōno chimed in. "I wonder if it's true?"

"It's true," said Akiyama. "The practice was called communal marriage. All the parents, in their generation, were husbands and wives, and their children, in their generation, were all husbands and wives. Of course there were times when couples who liked one another stayed together as an exclusive pair, but the rest were in effect free. That's why children knew only their mothers and only a matriarchal family existed. The system of monogamous marriage came about when private property began to predominate over communal property, and it became crucial to have an undisputed heir. So men began to keep a close watch on the fidelity of their wives."

"Ancient times sound pretty good. You must lend me that book." Like all Japanese husbands, Ōno enjoyed showing off his interest in other women in front of his wife.

"Engels would be no match for Ōno," Kaizuka sneered.

Tsutomu remained quiet, his head bowed. His own affairs bordered on a kind of communal marriage. Male students frequently swapped women with no particular feelings of jealousy. In spite of their attitude, Tsutomu did not think it was a good practice at all. It simply wasn't pleasant.

Some friends had urged him to take a look at the book by Engels under discussion. But when he reached the part in the preface that stated it was natural for there to be periods of cannibalism when the food supply was uncertain, he could not go on. He knew from his own experience at the front in Burma how men had to stifle a guilty conscience in order to eat human flesh. It was his agony to realize that cannibalism was the inevitable outcome of human nature.

Tsutomu couldn't have cared less if the system of monogamy was natural or unnatural. He was still at an age when he had no desire to possess everything, let alone a wife. And he certainly did not want to approve the justification of primitive cannibalism. Inferring from the logic of his emotions, he found absolutely no justification for thinking that just because ancient people acted in a certain manner that modern people had to behave the same way.

He had known the loneliness of a child abandoned by a mother who flees her home, and so adults who could discuss relations between a husband and a wife so flippantly repelled him. And he took it as a personal insult that Akiyama was denigrating the system of monogamy in front of his own wife's cousin.

"What's the matter?" Tomiko said to him. "You're disagreeably silent tonight." He raised his eyes to find her face unexpectedly close to his. But he did not detect the flirtatiousness he detested.

All evening he had enjoyed watching her work faithfully, bringing in the meal. With no time to flirt, her pleasant nature and the easy charm of the coquette showed through.

He smiled at her. He assumed that Tomiko would not understand the reason for his silence, but in any case the sympathy in her face was not unpleasant to him.

As it turned out, she had not been amused by the men's talk. She had brought a fair dowry and pin money with her when she was a bride. Someone in her position had little need for concern on the subject of monogamy. What rankled her was the tone of the discussion, which somehow seemed an affront to her womanly self-respect.

Tsutomu was right not to detect any coquetry in her expression. Given her emotions at the moment, she had no need to flirt.

She handed Tsutomu a sake cup and brought it together with her own. This was within the range of flirting that Ōno usually permitted. She did this with Tsutomu almost out of instinct, but her action disappointed him. What's more, he did not like sake.

Tomiko said, "You probably learned to hold your liquor during the war, didn't you, Tsutomu."

"Soldiers like me hardly ever got to drink liquor," he replied curtly.

The adult conversation was continuing. Akiyama was talking.

"I've heard that Eskimo husbands lend their wives to travelers. Now that's refreshingly openhearted. Maybe that's the true essence of human sexuality."

"I'm not sure about that," Kaizuka countered. "It may be an acquired feeling that developed from the need to maintain the social group. Before the birth of the nation-state there was a danger that the group might be destroyed if a husband's jealousy was not controlled."

"I have a tough time following such difficult ideas. But tell me, Akiyama, would you be willing to lend Michiko to, say... Kaizuka?" It was Ōno speaking now. He had started to say "to Tsutomu" but checked himself. Akiyama looked displeased.

"That's terrible," Tomiko interceded. "How about you? Would you give me to Kaizuka?"

Kaizuka's face turned red. Ōno flinched for a second, then burst out laughing.

"Don't be ridiculous! He'd turn down an old hag like you!"

Akiyama noticed that when Tomiko said "to Kaizuka" she was looking at Tsutomu.

Ōno looked over at Tomiko and gestured slightly with his eyebrows. That was their agreed signal that dinner was over. Tomiko went out, but came right back in mumbling, "It's heavy, it's heavy." She was carrying a tray lined with rows of items she had brought from the next room—bars of soap manufactured at Ōno's factory.

"Listen, Kaizuka," said Ōno, "these are a gift, but the other half are samples. If your union members want them, then collect a thousand yen and I'll have them delivered. Twenty yen per bar is enough for me. You can sell the rest for whatever you want."

Kaizuka at last realized the true purpose of tonight's dinner party. He smiled ruefully and said, "I won't take a commission." He picked up a sample, scratched it with a fingernail, and complimented Ōno by saying, "It's nice." Ōno's marketing was haphazard, but his company manufactured a good product.

Akiyama and Tsutomu were both asked to recommend the soap to the cooperative union at their college. This was a new method Ōno had hit upon for selling his product. Competition had gradually increased even for items like soap, and Ōno was no longer selling his product left and right as he had previously.

During a lull in the conversation, just as dinner was about to break up, Tomiko asked Tsutomu to tutor Yukiko in English. She had a hard time getting Ōno's consent. He generally agreed to everything his wife asked, but this time he was concerned, wondering aloud, "What will Michiko say?" But Tomiko reassured him by saying, "I've already spoken with her." With that the matter was settled.

Tsutomu, who stayed at Michiko's house that night, heard the couple talking in muffled voices for a long time in the next room. Akiyama was angry that Michiko had agreed to the arrangement without consulting him. Michiko said that she had neither agreed nor disagreed, but that Tomiko had decided on her own. She related the gist of their daytime conversation, and added that because she was Tsutomu's closest relative it wasn't right for him to live at Ōno's house, especially when there were so many empty rooms in this house. Of course Akiyama was dead set against this, but then Michiko pointed out that a scandal would surely arise between Tomiko and Tsutomu. This was a decisive point, and Akiyama unexpectedly softened, agreeing to take Tsutomu into his home.

"It can't be helped, I guess," he said. "Tomiko's whims have put us in a bind."

Akiyama had been staring at the ceiling the whole time.

Chapter 4

Koigakubo

Yukiko was a third-grader at a nearby Catholic elementary school. With her large frame and dark complexion, she resembled her father. When guests came to their house, she never failed to ask, "Who do you like best, Papa or Mama?"

On the third day after Tsutomu moved to Michiko's house he began helping with Yukiko's studies. At that time Yukiko asked him the question she put to all the other guests. Flustered, Tsutomu answered, "I like your Papa." He was a little shocked at the spiteful expression on the face of this child who was usually so innocent.

"Is that right? I prefer Mama."

When Tsutomu asked why she preferred her mother, Yukiko gave him the following reason.

Once, as part of her homework, she was assigned the project of coming up with a riddle. Ōno, who was drunk at dinnertime, taught her one. The question: What was the first thing Jesus said after he was born? The answer: "Waaaah!" The next day the teacher scolded Yukiko, and ever since then it was, "I hate Papa!"

Ōno did not have any profane intent. He told Yukiko the jokes he heard at the office out of sheer carelessness. His constant insensitivity had wounded the child in various ways, which explained why Yukiko disliked him.

Tsutomu noticed that Yukiko did not give any positive reasons for preferring Tomiko. Since he himself had grown up a stepson, he was sensitive to the reactions of a child to a careless mother, and decided not pursue the matter. He began to grow fond of his pupil.

Their lessons were held three times a week on those days when Tsutomu's afternoon lectures finished early. In the evenings, after eating the dinner Tomiko prepared for him, he would return to Michiko's house. Michiko was bothered that Tsutomu depended on Tomiko in this way, but Akiyama made it abundantly clear that he was happy his responsibility for Tsutomu's board had decreased, and so she could say nothing about the matter.

Akiyama set a number of conditions for taking in Tsutomu. First, Tsutomu would pay the same amount for board that he had been paying previously to the fam-

33

ily of his friend. Next, he could not bring home any girlfriends. Finally, he definitely had to attend school. This last condition was meant to keep Tsutomu from being alone frequently in the house with Michiko.

Michiko had never thought so lovingly about her dead father as when she heard these stipulations. Still, she accepted them all. Tsutomu was a little surprised by the serious expression on her face when she informed him about them. He took her earnestness simply as a sign that she wanted to save him from his dissolute lifestyle.

Michiko's self-respect was further wounded when she learned that the monthly fee Tomiko paid Tsutomu for tutoring Yukiko was equal to what Tsutomu paid Michiko for his board. Ōno agreed to pay such a large amount for tutoring in order to show his appreciation for all the help he had received from Michiko's father when he was young. But Michiko, being a woman, interpreted Ōno's willingness to pay Tsutomu so much as entirely Tomiko's doing. So Michiko, to restore her self-respect, juggled her household budget, which was not all that extravagant, and sent various things to Yukiko behind Akiyama's back.

Tsutomu knew nothing about Michiko's concerns. He had grown weary of his past life, and had come to Hake out of lingering affection for his cousin from the old days. It all seemed like a perfectly natural thing to do. At his age he took everything to be his emotional entitlement. It wasn't that he hadn't foreseen the subtle discord that inevitably arose between himself and Akiyama. He just thought that he could manage that discord if he hid his own dislike of Akiyama. Little did he dream that Akiyama would be especially attentive to the way Tsutomu's eyes were always following Michiko.

Truth be told, Tsutomu admired Michiko. Reappraising her through the eyes of a young man who has abandoned the indifference of childhood familiarity, he appreciated anew her innocent beauty, which had not changed over the years. He was especially charmed by the absence of anything superfluous in her movements. When she had nothing to do, she remained perfectly poised. And she never spoke needlessly.

He had acquired his sensitivity to precision and economy in movement on the battlefield, where actions were either required or prohibited, with nothing in between.

He had also acquired the habit of scrutinizing movement in general. For example, he observed the action of the spring water in the garden. The clear water gurgled as it flowed and constantly rolled pebbles along the bottom of the stream. He would kneel on the bank and gaze intently as a single pebble rolled two or three times, stopped, moved a little more, then suddenly tumbled twelve or fifteen centimeters, gradually making its way downstream. He would investigate just how far the current of water could move an inanimate stone in, say, ten minutes.

When he was a boy Tsutomu had been fond of the road that cut across the base of the slope. But his way of appreciating its beauty was out of the ordinary. He was moved more by the beauty he discovered in tracing the natural shape of the terrain than the beauty he saw in the contrasting light and shade of the chestnut groves and the woods of various trees that adorned the hillside. The route of the road indicated how people who traversed the hillside had saved themselves effort and useless motion.

The road rose a little in front of Chōsaku's house at Hake, then continued in a straight line on a gentle downward slope as far as the stone fence on the terrace of Ōno's house. From there it meandered through the mixed-growth forest on the hillside.

To the right were dry-cultivated fields. Further ahead, where the black earth planted in upland rice and greens spread out, the road descended to the narrow paddies that lined both sides of the Nogawa. On the opposite bank it gradually rose again. Farmhouses and the residences of city people dotted the landscape. Trees surrounded all the houses, and the land undulated gently as far as the pine grove at Tama Cemetery.

Some people from the city had built homes on lots created by leveling parts of the hillside. In the chestnut groves, where the underbrush had been cleared away, the light green flowers of the upper branches piled up over the darker green of the leaves. Evacuees had cleared the slope of trees in order to build their houses, and they had converted the land into broad, dry-cultivated fields surrounded by hedges. The road, following the contours of the hill, inclining gently up or down, widened at some points and narrowed at others. There was a graceful elegance in its movement as it held to the slope all along the way. Tsutomu followed it.

The road passed below an embankment of the light railway used to carry gravel from Tamagawara. Here it diverged from the slope for the first time. Crossing a swamp in the Nogawa basin, which narrowed suddenly in this vicinity, it turned to the right into a grassy plain that had dried out in the sun. Red pines grew scattered in the spaces among the young shrubs, not yet two or three feet tall, that formed a thicket.

Whenever he had walked over to visit Hake before he was drafted, this entire area had been forested, and the autumn foliage of the oak and sumac had been beautiful. Tsutomu remembered that when he entered the forest, no matter where he was, he felt as if he was going out in a boat into the boundless offing. The forests had been cleared for firewood, which was in short supply during the war, and for the timber needed to build the nearby airfield.

A small portion of the forest remained to the south of the vacant grassy plain. Zelkova and oak could be seen towering in the midst of the light green spreading low to the ground. Tsutomu proceeded to cut across the plain where there was no road.

It was cool in the forest. White and yellow flowers of the orchid family

35

bloomed in the undergrowth. A narrow path, well marked in some spots and not so well marked in others, unexpectedly crossed the forest through the underbrush. Sunlight fell on the underbrush in patches, amid the piles of leaves from the previous autumn.

Memories of the mountains in Burma flooded back to him. Tropical jungles drop their leaves with no regard to season, and the forest paths are narrow. When he was in Burma, Tsutomu often recalled the forests of Musashino. Now, in this June forest of Musashino, he thought of the lush jungles of Burma.

Tsutomu sat down on the grass. Except for the singing of a bird hidden in the upper branches far above, there was no sound. He took a deep breath.

"One lives freely in the mountains and forests." He recalled this line of a Meiji era poet. Tsutomu, who had wandered solitary in the tropical wilds, knew how frightening freedom could be. The harmony of the pleasant green of the oaks that had played the muse for the Meiji poet now looked to Tsutomu like nothing more than firewood. He could not imagine that an oak could grow so luxuriantly without the aid of human beings.

He suddenly straightened up. There was no particular reason for this. He had recently picked up the habit of moving his body meaninglessly in this way.

He stood. Walking deeper into the woods, he saw a small steel mass along the side of the path, the wreck of a tank. The treads were red with rust, the armored belly covered by graffiti scrawled in white chalk. Some kind of compressed gas canister had been tossed to the ground beside it.

His eyes glanced around. It looked as though the forest had come to an end. The bright rays of sunlight were shining between the tree trunks. As he walked along, the shimmering play of light and shadow was dizzying.

He came out onto a field. The broad surface of the land leveled out, exposing pebbles and red clay. In the distance beyond the ambiguous undulations of the field, two piles of earth squatted like humps, the red soil of their tops eroded by the rain. There was a single hut in ruins, its glass and mortar broken and scattered. These were the remains of an airport that had been constructed at the very end of the war.

Tsutomu cut leisurely across the despoiled landscape. He headed toward a spot at the opposite corner of the field where reds and yellows had congealed within the green of the forest. He did not understand what those colors were until he approached them and could see they were old flowerbeds.

In a run-down, Western-style garden, red and yellow roses were in full bloom. Through a lack of cultivation, they had returned to a wild state. Primroses crawled out from beneath hedges of plane trees and spread all over the narrow path. There was no sign on a gate that opened onto the interior of the forest. Roses grew on a trellis woven from thin bamboo.

A new, broader road led from the gate, passed through young cryptomeria, and descended once again to the Nogawa basin. The volume of water in the river had increased noticeably in just a short distance, and it flowed swiftly and deeply between banks enclosed by boards and stakes. The basin was narrow, and the heavy flow of spring water formed a pond. The well-built road crossed straight through some marshy land and over to the opposite shore, which approached to within twenty meters.

A rough wire fence surrounded the woods on the opposite side. At a turn in the road there was a single wooden gate that also had no sign on it. The road narrowed in front of the gate, continued along the fence, then ascended on a diagonal course.

The wooden gate clearly suggested that someone owned the flowerbeds. For some reason Tsutomu imagined that the owners were ancient nobility.

Climbing along the fence to the top of the rise, he came to a chestnut grove. As he passed through a sparse stand of trees, a concrete building like a gigantic factory came into view. Many small glass windows were lined up in rows high atop the building. He thought it a bit mysterious that the windows were not reflecting the slanting light of the sun, but as he drew a little closer he saw that the panes of glass were all missing.

The road, asphalted with shards of hard, blue-white stones, ran along the wire fence that extended from the wooden gate below. He followed it until the road passed through a large gate with a thatched roof. A lone charcoal-powered automobile had stopped there. The driver was reading a newspaper.

There was no sign on this gate either. He asked the driver who lived here. The man made an indignant face, as if to say "Don't you know?" then mentioned the name of a certain aviation company president who had been famous during the war.

The factory site ended at a building that resembled a warehouse. There was no one around. A strip of zinc roofing had come loose and was rattling in the evening breeze.

An oak forest descended along the hillside there, a path formed by nature bordering its outer edge. Tsutomu crouched down in the forest.

Apart from the inauspicious rasping of the zinc roof, he could hear nothing else. In the spaces where the soft green of the young oaks mingled, the sky was gradually beginning to darken. Tsutomu's heart was wounded.

On the way home, the mountains were clearly visible through an opening in the slope made by the light railway. Beyond the line of hills in Tama, which carried with them the same evanescent quality as the green of the tropics, the Tanzawa massif appeared low in the distance. It thrust up from the intricate group of mountaintops at Chichibu to the right, and dropped at an acute angle to a flat plain on the south slope of Ōyama. Thick clouds gathered at the top of the Tanzawa range and obscured Mt. Fuji.

On a different day, Tsutomu walked through the shield-shaped plateau across from the Nogawa, going as far as Fuchū. The old road he chose to take was intertwined all along the way with a new highway built for cars. The cross of a white chapel gleamed in the facilities built for the former Tachikawa airfield. It looked like someone conducting a fire drill. A thin rainbow over the water rose in a high arc into the sky.

A red fence surrounded a temple compound. The trunks of old zelkova trees, which were planted in a row here, were thickly gnarled. Foreign-made cars were constantly running along a road lined with old taverns.

Michiko would gaze in awe at Tsutomu whenever he returned from one of his walks, utterly lost in thought. This was not the lonely stepchild she had known from the old days. Something she did not understand had entered the heart of this quiet young man. She was not sure if the change was due to his experience in the war, but it certainly frightened her.

The change was apparent in his very actions. For example, there was his habit of going straight to his room without saying a word. She had never seen that behavior before.

When Akiyama was away, the two of them had long talks. They spoke mainly about their memories of Michiko's father, and it pleased Michiko that at such moments Tsutomu reverted to the quiet youth of old and felt nostalgic for the elder Miyaji as if he were his own father.

They each had their fathers' faces, and so they resembled one another nearly like a brother and sister. Facing one another on the veranda, they had the feeling at times that they were seeing what their own faces would look like if they were of the opposite sex. Their mutual regard bordered on self-admiration.

They were not able to talk about the elder Miyaji when they were at the dinner table with Akiyama, since he would usually fall into a silent funk. When the meal was over, he would immediately retreat to his study to translate or to prepare his lectures. After he had withdrawn, they would put on fresh tea and chatter away for a long time in the family room. One evening Akiyama scolded Michiko for this. It hurt Michiko to bring the matter up with Tsutomu the following morning, but she was relieved to see, contrary to her expectations, that he simply laughed it off, stood up, and left without so much as an unpleasant face.

Akiyama took Tsutomu's nonchalance as merely an expression of scorn and indifference. Michiko, on the other hand, read it as an act of kindness toward her. To show her gratitude, she began to do things for Tsutomu, and over time these things became her main everyday concern.

She also did her best for Akiyama. In all her efforts to please him there was a sentimentality that went beyond the reserve of a wife who had one of her relatives living in her house. Akiyama was surprised by Michiko's unexpected kindness. Had he known that her kindness was just an extension of her feelings for Tsutomu, he might have been a little more vigilant. Because his vigilance focused for the most part on Tsutomu's relationship with Tomiko, he was unable to grasp the significance of the change in his own wife.

For her part, Michiko gradually relaxed her watchfulness over the relationship between Tsutomu and Tomiko. This was the positive effect of the emotions she felt during her recent conversations with Tsutomu. It is believed that this type of emotion usually gives birth to jealousy, but for a simple heart like Michiko's, emotions worked in the opposite way. And in Tsutomu's case, she had not been mistaken.

His feelings for Tomiko did not go beyond the natural reaction young men in general have toward a woman who shows a liking for them. There is a tendency in novels to depict this kind of reaction as a motive for love; but in reality, if a man has no secret desire to exploit a woman's show of friendliness, then nothing will come of it. And Tsutomu lacked that secret desire.

It was hard to determine the precise limits of Tomiko's regard for Tsutomu. She had asked him to be Yukiko's tutor, but certainly something more than her usual capriciousness was involved. She could only express her feelings for Tsutomu through the typical mannerisms of a coquette, as she had at the dinner for Kaizuka. Her flirting was a daily necessity, like eating; but it had no significance, and so it remained uncertain whether she would push her flirtation to some end. The steps she had taken so far suggested that she did not intend anything further. Nonetheless, when she got up from the dinner table, she sometimes tottered a little, placing her hand on Tsutomu's shoulder. She did not display this kind of flirtation to just anyone.

Akiyama was sensitive to this kind of display by Tomiko. He limited his visits to her house to those days when Tsutomu was not tutoring Yukiko. He noticed that she did not listen as attentively to his conversation as she had before. The simple explanation for such inattention was that there was a limit to the energy even Tomiko could devote to flirting. But he was suspicious and worried that his own opinions concerning the decriminalization of adultery might legitimize the feelings he imagined Tomiko had for Tsutomu. He had not forgotten the way she looked at Tsutomu when she cut in on the discussion about lending a wife to another man.

The vexing thing for Akiyama was that because of Tomiko's capriciousness, he had no grounds on which to oppose Tsutomu staying at his house. He had had to put up with various things from the elder Miyaji. Now he thought of himself as fainthearted for putting up with a similar situation all over again for the sake of a woman he had fallen for. Taking advantage of Michiko's reserve toward him, he began to take pleasure in bullying her.

Because a husband's bad temper is frequently just a common feature of a household, a wife can usually ignore it. But when a husband comes to take pleasure in his temper, he hurts his wife. Without knowing the true motives of her husband, Michiko suffered because she assumed that his bad moods were caused by her cousin living with them. One evening she wondered if she shouldn't find some excuse to have Tsutomu quit as Yukiko's tutor and move back to his former residence at the house of his friend. She surprised herself when she realized that she felt absolutely no inclination to make him leave. She shuddered when she imagined what life at Hake would be like after Tsutomu had gone.

She considered confiding in Ōno about the situation and asking him to take Tsutomu into his home, but she did not care for that course of action either. Now that she had come to trust Tsutomu, there was no reason to fear a scandal with Tomiko. She examined her own feelings—why it was she did not want to send Tsutomu to Tomiko's house—and she came to understand just how important he had become to her.

She understood that the pleasant talks she had with him when Akiyama was not around, that looking at his face, listening to his voice, hearing the sound of his footsteps or some sign of movement even when they were in separate rooms, had become connections her life could not do without. It occurred to her that she was always thinking about him while she worked in the kitchen, even when he was not home.

She had had similar feelings in her life, when she had been absorbed in her brothers, or in Akiyama during their engagement period. She tried to compare her emotions then with her emotions now, but found it extremely difficult to call up her memories.

The feelings she had for Tsutomu resembled love, but since she would not permit herself to call it that, it was premature to conclude that she was in love. She had never really been in love before, and the novels she had read depicting the emotion made her think it happened only to other people and had no connection to her.

Akiyama's increasingly intense irritableness and Michiko's suffering did not escape Tsutomu's attention. He knew full well that this was all due to him. He had a young man's sensitivity, and he recognized the true reason for Akiyama's bad mood. His sympathy for Michiko grew, but he did not feel like speaking to her about Akiyama's motives. He was afraid of hurting Michiko. At the same time, he was afraid of his own ulterior motives. If he criticized Akiyama, he might be able to profit from the situation and take Akiyama's place beside Michiko.

Leaving Hake would be the easy thing to do. Now, however, he thought he should not abandon Michiko to her faithless husband. He decided that he had to risk everything, that he had to do the best he could as an ally of Michiko. Examining his decision more closely, it is readily apparent that it was an expression of his love for Michiko. Considering his proven aptitude for the sexual conquest of the women he had known at school, he could have easily taken Tomiko any time—if that had been his aim. So long as he was near Michiko, he had no desire for that.

In this way he entered into what might be called a state of war with Akiyama. Since he was effectively powerless, he intently avoided contact with the enemy. To the extent possible, he would not show himself to Akiyama. He also would not speak to Michiko in front of Akiyama. When Akiyama was away he made up for his silence by being kind to Michiko. It goes without saying that his situation resembled that of a paramour.

He wanted to share with Michiko the love he had for the natural beauty of Hake. Through his reading he had become increasingly knowledgeable about the topography of the neighborhood. In the evenings he would read in the study, where he could close himself off in order to avoid Akiyama. To make a room for him, they had opened up part of Miyaji's library and rearranged it so he could sleep there. Tomes on the history and geography of Musashino lined the bookcases of the old man, who had dabbled in the subject. Tsutomu had fallen into the habit of noting matters of topography after going off to the war, and so he read these books one after another, and learned a great deal about the original contours of Kokubunji, or the origins of the Musashino plateau.

He often invited Michiko along on his walks, and would tell her about the topography of the vicinity or the founding of a temple. Michiko, who had been raised at Hake, was of course accustomed to the natural surroundings of her house, and had even been absorbed in collecting butterflies when she was a child. Yet she knew far less than he did about local history and geography. She had an interest in learning more about the things she was accustomed to seeing. For all that, she put up with Tsutomu's occasionally tedious and pedantic explanations, listening until the end only because she enjoyed his voice.

The Nogawa, which flowed in front of Hake, held special interest for Tsutomu. Consulting a 5,000:1 scale map that, unsurprisingly, Miyaji had in his possession, Tsutomu discovered that this small river was the upper current of a larger one he had once seen below the heights at Seijō Academy when he had been in high school. This river flowed below the house of his friend in Den'en Chōfu, where he stayed before he came back to Hake. The river was six meters wide at Seijō and Den'en Chōfu, and, like a drainage canal, swiftly carried an abundance of water all out of proportion to its width. This water was the runoff of irrigated rice paddies from Kamata all the way to Rokugō.

The Nogawa was only about two meters wide along the front of Hake. Hardly any bridges crossed this current as it ran through the rice fields. Here too the water flowed in an abundance out of proportion to the river's width. According to the map, the river started below the railroad embankment in the vicinity of Kokubunji station. It appeared to come from the hillside adjoining Hake, collecting the spring water there. Tsutomu thought it unnatural that in a distance of less than two kilometers the volume of water should increase so much.

One day, when Akiyama had a faculty meeting and planned to be home late, Tsutomu invited Michiko to go with him and search for the source of the river. The road did not run precisely along the river, and because Tsutomu planned to investigate the amount of spring water that flowed out from the slope at Hake, they decided to take the road that ran along the base of the hillside.

It was a muggy, cloudy afternoon that hinted at the approach of the rainy season. Along the way Michiko listened, as she always did, to Tsutomu's rambling explanations of the geography of the region. They sounded like music to her. She could not follow his explanations, which demonstrated a defeated soldier's attention to the details of topography, but it was a pleasure for her to listen to anything that was so close to his heart.

A deserted stillness hung over the road, which meandered beneath the tall zelkova and oak trees decorating the hillside. The stillness was broken occasionally by the sound of water. Water from an unknown source on the slope made a furious roar as it began its descent, flowing past the road in the direction of the Nogawa. The dancing play of the water was like some living thing as it passed the road and reached level ground.

All along the road were houses with Western-style red roofs and farmhouses surrounded by hedges. As they walked on for some distance, the houses were spaced farther and farther apart. Climbing the slope a short distance, the road leveled out again and headed into a stand of cryptomeria. A fence of Tama stone about a meter high had been built on the side of the mountain, indicating there were residences above.

The water again crossed the road and descended. Under a small stone bridge, which was curved like a bridge in a temple, rocks were arranged as in a garden, and the water leapt down between them. Michiko judged that the plot of land belonging to the mansion here extended from the road over the entire slope of the mountain. Observing that the rocks and the stand of cryptomeria were properly arranged all the way down to where the slope ended at a level field, Michiko felt that the elegant taste of the mansion's owner was out of place.

The Nogawa basin was very narrow in this area, and bamboo groves bordered the river on the opposite bank. The water flowed just as abundantly as it did at Hake, and could be clearly seen even at a distance.

Beyond the stand of cryptomeria, the stream cut across the road more frequently. The water would suddenly emerge from the shade of the bamboo groves or from the base of the stone fences, then flow parallel to the road.

Accompanied by the shape of the current and the rhythm of its sound, their feet moved in harmony with nature.

The water poured into a pond. There was a sign for a fishing canal, but they saw no customers. The water was a stagnant blue with no sign of any fish. It flowed out from a corner of the pond, and turned once more in the direction of the Nogawa River. There was a shrine on the side of the mountain, separating the road from the pond. The water continued its descent alongside the stone steps.

To visit the source of the water, they proceeded to the interior of the shrine. They could follow the current as far as the back of a prayer hall surrounded by a horse-shoe-shaped cliff. As it did in the spring at Hake, the water bubbled up as though crawling out over a spot where the black earth of the cliff, on which grass was growing, met the flat surface of the grounds of the shrine. The water spread out beneath the veranda of the prayer hall and ran along the low cliffs on both sides, creating a natural channel as it descended.

Michiko felt compelled to ask Tsutomu, who was standing there gazing intently at the shape of the water gushing out, "What do you admire so much about that?"

Michiko was caught up in his interest in the water. She concentrated on the sound she heard coming from above the cliff to the left of the shrine. The water burbled as it cascaded down. Clearly the water was originating higher than the spring water at the back of the temple. A separate, furious roaring from below overlay the burbling from above.

Michiko drew Tsutomu's attention to that sound. She felt proud that she had been able to contribute something to his topographical studies.

They climbed from the side of the prayer hall along a small, zigzag path in the middle of a grove of zelkova trees. They came out onto a flat area where the trees thinned. A large road was unexpectedly close. People were passing on bicycles.

A concrete gutter about thirty centimeters wide ran beside some houses on the edge of the forest, and the water came rushing from the direction of the road. At the spot where the slope began, the gutter was inclined at an angle of fifteen degrees. The water bounced against the sides, gurgling as it slid along. A louder noise rose from the depths of a bamboo grove ahead.

The gutter was obviously connected to the overflow of a water supply called the Tamagawa Josui, which lay beyond the rail lines. This meant that the main current of the Tamagawa was in fact the source, and was responsible for creating the impression that the Nogawa had an unnaturally abundant volume of water. Tsutomu looked back at Michiko, and laughed with satisfaction.

"It's just as I thought," he said. "It's drawing from the Tamagawa Josui."

Michiko wanted to hug Tsutomu, who seemed so happy.

They went back through the zelkova woods to the side of the shrine and came out on the road below. Passing a roadside teahouse that stood next to the *torii* gate of the shrine, they walked on for some distance. Water gushed forth like falls in the gaps between the groves and dug out deep channels that crossed under the road.

They climbed a gentle incline to some open fields. A branch of the water retreated gently to the right along the slope, and a road descended, crossed a small bridge below the confluence of the Nogawa, and headed toward a cryptomeria forest far ahead on the opposite bank.

Tsutomu, standing on top of the bridge, was surprised that the water of the Nogawa was as abundant as ever.

The railroad embankment, which was marked on the map as the source of the water, bounded the edge of the basin in the distance. The large mouth of an open drainpipe appeared near an incline on the right-hand side. The sight of falling white water commanded the view.

"I see.... The source must be on the other side of the rail line," he said, laughing. Michiko was unable to share his joy. She was now preoccupied, wondering why she'd had the impulse to embrace Tsutomu a few minutes earlier when they were behind the temple. Her thoughts skirted around the word that identified the emotion she had been resisting for some time and did not want to acknowledge.

The river narrowed and the silt on the bottom gradually became visible. As they passed by a large road, the basin turned into narrow rice paddies; the river flowed close against the mixed-growth forests on the hillside; and a single path ran beside the river.

Climbing the railroad embankment, they came out on the opposite side where an unexpectedly broad basin stretched before them. More rice paddies had been developed there. Below them to the right the basin was bounded by the embankment of a branch rail line. There was a swamp where tall miscanthus grasses and reeds grew thickly. The water filled a large pond. Its overflow poured into earthen pipes, which appeared to be sucking the water into them. This was the source.

Descending along a path that cut diagonally across the embankment, they stood at the side of the pond. A middle-aged farmer was fiddling with the rice seedlings in the paddy. When he spotted them his face clearly showed his annoyance and antipathy.

"What's this place called?" Tsutomu asked.

"Koigakubo," the man answered brusquely.

Michiko felt as though her legs had lost their strength. Tsutomu had mentioned Koigakubo to her before. The Chinese character used to represent the syllables "koi" means a yearning love. In this case the character was used for its phonetic value only and had no connection to the original meaning of the place name. Koigakubo was recorded in an ancient legend about a warrior from Kamakura and a beautiful woman. The warrior went off to fight in the western provinces, and the woman, grieving for her lover, threw herself into this pond.

It seemed to her the name explicitly identified the yearnings she was now struggling to resist. Following the river upstream with Tsutomu in order to find its source, she had ended up at a place that made her self-conscious about the sudden impulse to hug Tsutomu she had felt on the way.

Her surroundings made her fearful. The embankments of the railway, which had divided into two tracks, blocked their field of vision. She felt trapped in this place.

A shabby two-car train careened by and turned onto the branch line. Its rumbling made her shiver.

She looked at the man she was now so drawn to. He stood there innocently, apparently still examining the source of the river he had finally found. Would she have to suffer this emotion alone?

A narrow drainage ditch was emptying water into the pond. The water was abundant and fast flowing. Tsutomu said he would go further upstream.

Farmhouses faced out onto the ditch. Michiko walked ahead of Tsutomu. He stopped to ask something of a farm wife who was washing vegetables. Michiko walked further ahead. She was no longer listening to Tsutomu, who caught up with her and droned on about what he had just learned. The water in this ditch was also drawn from the Tamagawa Josui, which meant that the source of both rivers, the Nogawa and the Tamagawa, was the same.

CHAPTER 5

CONCERNING THE FLIGHT OF BUTTERFLIES

When Michiko realized she was attracted to Tsutomu, her initial impulse was to try to control her emotions. Although she did not love her husband, she believed it was impermissible for a wife to have such feelings for another man, especially if the man was her cousin. Looking back over the history of her feelings for Tsutomu, she had treated him kindly, as if he was a younger brother. That he would now be the object of her affection seemed unspeakably ugly.

Michiko had never known the feeling of love. She had read about it in novels when she was a girl, but those stories almost always had frightening endings. She did not believe she had within her either the strength or the desire even to attempt such feelings.

She felt this way because, first of all, she did not consider her youthful propensity to dote on her husband the same as love.

She had lived in the shadow of her father continuously since childhood. The peaceful, proper atmosphere of the household created by the elder Miyaji, a successful descendant of samurai, was everything to her. Her marriage, her feelings for Tsutomu—so long as they were all contained within this atmosphere, she felt at peace. This habit of mind had not changed even after the death of her father.

The illicit love for Tsutomu she was so conscious of unexpectedly dragged her out of her peaceful existence.

Tsutomu noticed that she was silent all the way home from Koigakubo. He had no way of knowing the cause of her silence, but he figured she must be fatigued from the hike, or bored with his long-winded talks on topography. The considerate words he spoke from time to time as they walked along pierced her heart deeply.

The rainy season started. The days when she was trapped indoors and had to spend more and more time face-to-face with Tsutomu were fearful ones for Michiko. The kindness she had been able to show him earlier without feeling self-conscious was mingled now with the worry that he would see through her kindness.

Throughout all her suffering, she never once questioned whether she might be mistaken in thinking she was in love. This unquestioning attitude demonstrated the character of her heart. Nothing was more essential to Michiko than believing in herself.

It did not occur to her even to think of asking Tsutomu to leave Hake. She intended to control her emotions, but implicit in her self-confidence was the desire not to lose the pleasure of seeing Tsutomu every day. The exertions of her heart to suppress her love turned her everyday concerns even more toward love. And there is nothing as richly sustaining for love as common concerns.

During the two weeks they had been together, Michiko and Tsutomu had revived the habit of calling each other by their childhood names—Mit-chan and Tomu-chan. Tsutomu was surprised one day when she addressed him formally as Tsutomu. He mulled over the significance of the shadow of distress that flitted across her eyebrows at that moment. In the end he could not discover any meaning other than deference to Akiyama, who disliked her closeness to Tsutomu. He too abandoned the use of their childhood names, but this brought new distress for Michiko. They had talked to each other so many times, and this was the first time he had done something without telling her why. She forgot that she was the one who had failed to explain her behavior to him in the first place.

Communicating your feelings to someone you love, however, is unavoidable. Thus the strange way she avoided sitting face-to-face with him; the awkwardness she exhibited whenever she served him; the trembling of her hands when she brought him tea on those nights when he was in his room alone—all of these things impressed themselves upon this twenty-four-year-old man.

Initially, Tsutomu likewise denied his feelings. As with Michiko, his resistance was the result of the innocent familiarity he'd had with his cousin when they were children. He concluded that the discord between Michiko and her husband would only grow more serious if he continued to be looked after in this household. He secretly intended to do his best for Michiko's sake, but because his intentions became more of a burden for Michiko, his good will came to nothing.

One day he abruptly sat down in front of her.

"I was thinking it might be best for me to go back to my old lodgings," he said.

Michiko could not respond. She knew that Tsutomu had been wanting to tell her something. She had a vague notion of what he wanted to say, but she was afraid to hear it.

"Why? Is there something you don't like?"

She made this perfunctory reply, and then suddenly started to cry.

Her own selfish emotions did not allow her to be reasonable toward him. Thus it was painful to her to cause such feelings in him. Amid her tears Michiko found the courage for the first time to look Tsutomu straight in the face.

"Tsutomu, you're really worried about me, aren't you? But there's nothing to worry about. I know Akiyama hasn't made you feel welcome, but I'm willing to put up with anything if I can have you stay here with us. Even though things may be a little strange around here at times, please don't mind them." She smiled at him. "It'll be all right, won't it? From now on I'll do my best to be careful."

Tsutomu was moved by this. He had never doubted that Michiko was the only person who had ever cared for him, but he never thought she cared so much that he could cause her to cry. Then he realized that he had been harboring the unpleasant thought that he was unworthy of being treated kindly. Tears came to his eyes.

"But...isn't it wrong of me...."

"It's all right. After all, while you're teaching Yuki-chan, you can live here without using up your money. And when you graduate, you can work at Ōno's company."

"I couldn't care less about such things."

"That's not a proper attitude."

She went into endless detail about Tsutomu's future. She absolutely had to talk about this in order to keep the sentimentality out of their conversation.

Later that evening, as he was lying in bed and thinking things over, he could hardly misconstrue the significance of Michiko's attitude. This was only the second time in his adult life that he had seen Michiko cry because of him. The first was when he had shipped off to Burma. Comparing her expression today with her expression then, he detected a difference. The tears were the same. But the look in her eyes was different.

He had seen that look previously during their intimate talks together after he moved to Hake. He had taken it as an expression of her innocent joy and was glad that such gaiety had returned to Michiko. The surprise he felt at seeing that same expression when she had been crying earlier today came back to him now.

The connection he made between his surprise and the workings of his own heart, which to that point had been unconsciously scrutinizing Michiko's behavior, pleasantly stimulated the confidence he had gained from his affairs with those students he had met.

However, his regard for his cousin reasserted itself. It struck him as a defilement to presume that Michiko had within her the same decadent quality as those students. He took it as a sign of progress that he wanted to verify Michiko's difference by meeting one of his old lovers.

Of all his lovers, one was really peculiar. The ugliness of her dark skin and flat face didn't especially set her apart from her companions, but she was different in that she proclaimed an old-fashioned, sentimental love. She announced to everyone that she loved Tsutomu, and she often stared longingly at him. Tsutomu wanted to find out for sure whether or not the look in her eyes was the same as in Michiko's.

He went to a coffeehouse in Kanda where the woman and her companions hung out. He was met with harsh accusations. Presently the girl in question came strolling in with a man. She had just been to the graduation ceremony at the dressmaking school she attended, and was showing off a large diploma written in English. She laughed derisively at Tsutomu.

"You've fallen for your beautiful cousin," she said, "so I guess I've been dumped."

As she spoke, she looked at him through her rolled-up diploma, as if through a telescope. The single eye that gleamed within was blinding to Tsutomu.

As he left the coffee shop he wondered if he hadn't lost his edge, since he'd believed that such a woman might actually have a heart. The way she looked at me before meant absolutely nothing, he thought. Reconsidering the matter, perhaps he was making too much of the look in Michiko's eyes as well.

The words "you've fallen for your beautiful cousin" stuck in his mind. He stopped suddenly and stood still. Rumors have neither roots nor leaves, and of course he had not previously been conscious of his own feelings. Then it occurred to him: *Have I misinterpreted the look in Michiko's eyes? Because I'm hoping she's in love with me? Am I the one who's in love?*

On the train back to Koganei, Tsutomu kept turning this question over in his mind. Inside the packed, humid railcar, he chose to deny it; but once the train left Mitaka, as the number of passengers decreased, as the number of trees and fields outside the windows increased, and as he gradually approached Hake, his feelings changed. Carried along by the train, his feelings improved.

He thought he would get a definitive answer the moment he entered the house and came face-to-face with Michiko. But Michiko was out. The emptiness he felt at that moment was decisive.

This was the first time he'd ever felt he was in love. He thought that none of his previous affairs had had anything to do with love. Indeed, he had always scorned the idea. The thoughts and feelings he brought home with him from the battlefield left no room for such an emotion.

Am I really in love? he wondered as he entered his room. He was intoxicated by this great discovery, but there was still room for him to test his own feelings. In his mind he ran through all the changes in his emotions since he had come to Hake. The figure of Michiko in various guises and at various moments floated before him. These images of her were all so sweetly tinged that he believed they proved he had been in love with her for some time.

He recalled the times when he had visited the house at Hake as a boy and played with Michiko. Michiko had married when he was thirteen. He concluded that his memories of his closeness with Michiko all pointed to their future love.

Tsutomu saw their family relationship as a foundation for love. In contrast, Michiko felt that being Tsutomu's cousin was a hindrance. It might be possible, perhaps, to detect a difference in the feelings of men and women as they fall in love. Women instinctively know the difference between love and other emotions. For men it is possible to attribute the complexion of love to any emotional attachment. In that spirit, all feelings of affection resemble love a little.

Yet neither of them believed they had a physical desire for the other. Michiko shuddered in thrill and disgust at the idea that she would do with Tsutomu what she did with Akiyama. Even Tsutomu was too respectful of her to think of Michiko as a sexual object the way he thought of his former lovers. His premonitions frightened him.

Their love proceeded from the mutual realization that they themselves were in love. Such calculations might appear to work against the normal impulses of affection, but becoming aware of oneself is a surprisingly important first step for love, which is, after all, a product of culture.

Tsutomu had many questions. Would Michiko love him in return? Were the signs of love he thought he had glimpsed in her false? Once he believed he was in love, he began to lose confidence.

When Michiko came back from her shopping, she was, unfortunately for him, in a cheerful mood. Talking sentimentally with Tsutomu temporarily undid that mood. Her innocent smile cut Tsutomu. His sense of humiliation was mixed with despair.

For Tsutomu, his life was now colored in new hues. His days were divided into two parts. One was the pleasant time when he was either out or shut up alone in his room and thinking about Michiko. The other was the painful time he saw her and discovered proof to support his despair. As always, Michiko was kind to him, and her kindness hid the suffering of her love. Yet he could never tell for sure if she was in love with him. It was his habit to persist in something once he was convinced of it, and in any case, tormenting himself produced a most agreeable feeling.

What really hurt him was that Michiko showed the same kindness to Akiyama. For example, she used to bring a shoehorn to Tsutomu when he put on his shoes in the morning. Recently he had come to dislike this gesture. Without even trying to consider why he felt this way, he just decided that from now on he would quickly take the shoehorn himself before she could hand it to him. Then one day he saw Michiko give the shoehorn to Akiyama, and he finally realized why he had come to dislike her show of kindness so intensely. He hated it when Michiko did anything for him the same way she did for Akiyama. He realized that he felt the same sensation whenever she helped him on with his jacket or waited on him at the dinner table. In short, any wifely obedience on her part was extremely distasteful to him.

Since he harbored no hopes of Michiko, he was experiencing the misery of a paramour.

From time to time he wondered, *What am I going to do about her?* Again, he had never thought of her as an object of sexual desire. Thus, he shouldn't have felt dissatisfied living with her every day like this. *Perhaps I want her to love me. But if that's the case, what else do I want besides having her worry about me?* He was unable to answer this question conclusively.

Michiko noticed his fretfulness. It bothered her, seeing the worry in his eyes—a look she had never seen in him before. She could not comprehend his feelings, and so she thought perhaps he was struggling with the idea that he should leave Hake. In order not to reveal her own suffering to him, she decided to act cheerful. But no matter how hard she tried, somehow she could not quite carry it off. Her apprehension that next time she might lose Tsutomu added to her distress over her love for him.

Their behavior did not escape Akiyama's notice. He flattered himself that all this was the result of his own bad temper and the prelude to Tsutomu's departure.

Tomiko, on the other hand, saw right through their relationship—perhaps to a greater degree than even the two themselves were aware. Because of the sensitivity of a woman towards other women, she first noticed the change in Michiko's attitude. Michiko was suffering, but when Tsutomu was not around there was a charm in even her most trivial movements that had not been there before. Tomiko noticed in particular that Michiko was paying more attention to her makeup, which she had always used sparingly.

Tomiko also observed that whenever Tsutomu ate at her house he looked absentminded and stared at the wall. Whereas before he had always responded to her jokes in an easygoing manner, now he sometimes forgot to answer her. Whenever the subject of Akiyama came up, his expression changed.

Tomiko was the sort of woman who always assumed that, wherever there was a man and a woman, there would be love. She was especially receptive to the charms of Tsutomu, so it was natural for her to imagine a relationship between him and his beautiful cousin.

She correctly judged that the two of them did not yet realize their love for each other. She wanted to see them together in order to confirm her suspicion, and so one day, out of the blue, she dropped by Michiko's house for dinner. The dinner table was gloomy, and she was the only one who did any talking. She noticed that the two lovers did not even look at one another. Moreover, they would study each other whenever the other one was looking off somewhere else.

Tomiko thought there was love for every couple, and the power of her imagination made her jealous.

Once, as Akiyama was droning on to her yet again about the rationality of adultery, she laughed and pointed out that his argument might well be proven at his own house. Akiyama fell silent and left soon after. Tomiko, recalling his contorted features, laughed to herself.

It was wrong of her to laugh. Akiyama was genuinely angry. As he approached his house, his legs trembled and he sensed that something obscene had been going on there.

He was especially indignant toward Tsutomu. He thought it was indecent to allow such an immoral young man into his home. His indignation made him feel superior to Tsutomu. The anger this fake Stendhalian was experiencing at this moment marked the first time he had ever felt anything real.

The house was quiet. Michiko was in the family room; Tsutomu was in his room. It occurred to Akiyama that the two of them had just now gone to their separate places.

Michiko was startled by the fearsome look in Akiyama's eyes. This was a look she had never before seen in all their years of marriage.

He went into his study, barely able to suppress the impulse to push his wife away from him. Sitting among the mountain of documents that were the source of his livelihood, he slowly calmed down.

The dilemma facing him was how to determine if the relationship Tomiko had brought to his attention was real. Tomiko had only implied that it was suspicious. He tried to conjure up images of Tsutomu and Michiko. If someone said they looked suspicious, then of course they looked suspicious. But that was hardly definitive proof of an affair. And if nothing was going on between them, any display of sullenness in front of them would saddle him with the role of a foolish, jealous husband.

The husband in him thought the most important thing was not actually confirming whether there was something real between Tsutomu and Michiko, but whether their relationship had drawn the attention of others. He himself had not noticed until another person had pointed it out to him. He remembered with displeasure Tomiko's mischievous smile.

At the same time, he was aware that his attitude now was related to his own success or failure with Tomiko. He thought that for him to have left so soon and come back home was certainly a misstep on his part.

He thought that he did not love Michiko. Thus, the question for him was whether he ought to forgive Michiko's infidelity in order to justify his own claim to Tomiko. At the very least he had to pretend to forgive Michiko in front of Tomiko. Moreover, he realized that the relationship between Michiko and Tsutomu would eliminate Tsutomu as a serious rival for Tomiko. Thinking things over in this manner, he regained his composure.

Were they really having an affair? Selfishly, Akiyama put his faith in Michiko's fidelity.

Michiko was startled a second time by how calm her husband was when he reappeared in the family room. He even spoke gently to her—something he rarely did these days. Still, she could not forget the expression on his face when he had come back to the house a little while ago. As an unfaithful wife, she could sense the meaning in his expression, and so was unable to ask him what was wrong.

No matter what, she was in love with a man who was not her husband. But that man did not feel the same way toward her. In that respect, she was not being unfaithful. She was the only one in love, and that was her freedom. This thought made her sad about her feelings for the first time.

The rainy season ended. One Sunday the three of them were sitting out on the veranda. Recently Akiyama had begun to appear more often before Michiko and Tsutomu. Ironically, whenever Akiyama was present, the two of them could be more relaxed in each other's company.

The brilliant July sun shone down on the garden and sparkled on the surface of the pond. Miyaji had planted a kind of Japanese honeysuckle called coral tree. He had received the seedlings from an acquaintance in Kamakura. The plants surrounded the back of the pond, and the old man had loved how the color of the trunks had the luster of human skin.

They sat there quietly. Akiyama finally got up and went down to the garden, nonchalantly sidling back around to the veranda. When he reached a spot where he was no longer visible to the other two, he abruptly drew in under the eaves, hoping to overhear what they were talking about.

All he could hear was the screech of cicadas. The burbling of water grew louder as it flowed down from the spring, pooled in the pond, then tumbled farther below where narcissus, not yet in flower, grew in abundance.

He could not hear any voices on the veranda, but Akiyama could tell that they had not moved from their seats.

A small bird—he did not know what it was called—swooped down from the woods, shaking the leaves of one of the coral trees as it passed. The hollow of Hake, which had eaten deeply into the hillside, was a kind of pathway for birds. Every season birds from all around passed through the watershed between Musashino and Tama. They rustled the tops of the trees on the lower level of Hake.

Like the birds that traversed this area, butterflies also used the hollow as a pathway. Various butterflies—swallowtail, four-footed, cabbage—cut through the garden, alighting on the flowers blooming by the stream.

Today two swallowtails came flying in from the direction of the Nogawa, fluttering in a space about two meters off the ground. The wings of one were large and black; the wings of the other were light brown and thin.

The black butterfly was languidly fanning its wings. The light-brown butterfly stuck close beneath it, busily repeating its vertical movements as though trying to push upward. Each time it looked as though its head would touch the underside of the butterfly above it, its body would suddenly drop. Then it would press upward again.

All this time the black butterfly moved slowly and calmly. It seemed to be constantly suppressing the rise of the butterfly below. The two insects moved little by little toward the upper part of the pond; the busy flight of the insect beneath caused it to lag behind, creating a gap between them that determined the path of their flight.

The veranda remained quiet. Akiyama sensed that the Michiko and Tsutomu were watching the butterflies. He became intensely jealous.

Akiyama's intuition was on target, for they had been unable to take their eyes off the insects. The coral trees and the pond in the background were hazy. Only the two butterflies seemed to shine, as if floating before their eyes.

It occurred to them that the insects had paired off for mating, but since neither of them knew anything about butterflies, their judgments as to which was the male and which the female were completely opposite.

Michiko imagined that the butterfly underneath was the female. This butterfly, like herself, was embracing a painful one-sided love. Continuing on her fruitless journey, she was trying to escape from the large-hearted butterfly above. Tsutomu, however, was aware of her every emotion, and wherever her heart was going, he was there ahead of it.

Tsutomu thought that the butterfly below was the male. Like his heart, which was longing for Michiko, the butterfly would reach for the one above, only to be thoughtlessly rejected each time and forced to retreat. It was compelled to repeat its painful efforts over and over.

Akiyama abruptly appeared in their field of vision, running towards the pond, hands raised, chasing the butterflies. The two of them awoke from their reverie. The butterflies separated, rose higher in the air, came back together again, and, entangled once more, flew off toward the Nogawa.

Michiko thought that Akiyama's thin arms, flailing and bare to the elbows, were ugly.

Tsutomu and Michiko's gaze met. There was no doubt about the significance of their gleaming eyes.

CHAPTER 6

A MIDSUMMER NIGHT'S DREAM

Tsutomu left the house alone. His eyes searched after the butterflies, which had flown off, but he couldn't locate them. He saw only the empty fields spread before him, broiling in the July heat. The torrid sun on his forehead felt good as he walked along the road that followed the contours of the hillside at Hake.

Akiyama's display of jealousy had given him the chance to observe Michiko's true feelings. He felt a strength throughout his body. It was a sensation of power that he had never imagined could exist in him. This sensation was the exultation of a young man who has captured for the first time the heart of a woman he loves. That he should feel that joy as a kind of strength was characteristic of a demobilized soldier.

He of course figured that there would be no obstacles to realizing this love. He was not interested in adultery the way Akiyama was, but he was caught up suddenly in the illusion that he was surrounded by pairs of men and women bound together by a stupid yoke called marriage.

As an unhappy child abandoned by his mother, he was far removed from the nonsense of spoiled, ignorant young men who claim that they hate the institution called "family". At the very least, for him, a family possessed a hardness that was a crystallization of all the envy he felt when he was young.

Now he found himself in the position of home wrecker because of his love for Michiko. She was someone else's wife, and he was startled to think that a family was so fragile it could shatter with a single push. He had watched many husbands die tragically at the battlefront grieving over their wives and children. One man said to him when he died, "If by any chance you get back, don't let my wife know I died like this." By bringing misfortune to all, even a government can destroy families in this way. Why should his own passion, which at least brought happiness to himself, be considered wrong, even if it broke up a home?

He recalled the defense of adultery that Akiyama had rehearsed at Tomiko's house that night. *He would panic if his own house were on fire, but he goes ahead and presents his really strange theories,* Tsutomu thought. *I must admit, however, I haven't found any flaws in his argument. If he really believes what he says, then he has no right to object to my emotional bond with Michiko. He ought to divorce her. Then we can be together.*

Tsutomu halted and sat in the shade of a roadside tree. The incessant screech of large brown cicadas filled the green of the trees and the groves over the hillside. Staring at a line of ants strenuously carrying their food across the dry red soil before him, he turned over and over in his mind the good fortune he would have if he lived with Michiko.

It did not seem there was any way for things to turn out so smoothly. Akiyama was definitely trying to win Tomiko over with all his talk about how irrational the system of monogamy was. But unless Tomiko divorced Ōno and married Akiyama, Akiyama would never let Michiko go. An academic always reasoned like that. In the end all their calculations came down to doing what was best for them.

But I'm only thinking about myself as well–I don't care. Do I have to look after other people?

He stood up. As he started to walk back to the house, it occurred to him that the relationship between Michiko and him had not progressed to the point where they could talk about marriage or divorce. They had not even reached the point where they had confessed their love. He merely thought he had detected in Michiko's eyes a sign of the passion he himself felt. He laughed.

This is strange. It seems certain that she loves me, but I don't know what she's trying to do. I can't tell just from her eyes if her love is strong enough to abandon Akiyama. I'm going to have to find a way to make sure.

His feelings for Michiko caused him to leap ahead to the prospect of an exclusive union with her. Given the history of their intimacy to this point, a life based on love was inconceivable in any form other than an exclusive union.

However, as he got closer to the house, he began to feel more and more appalled by his own ardor. He was frightened by the difficulty of saying the word "love" to Michiko. By the time he entered the front gate, he had begun to have doubts. Hadn't he been mistaken about what he detected for an instant in Michiko's eyes?

While Tsutomu was out on his walk, Akiyama and Michiko had a decisive exchange. Akiyama seized the opportunity provided by Tsutomu's decision to go out without saying anything to them. Like any academic, Akiyama knew how to express himself quietly. But in this case he demanded from her a clear answer as to whether or not she loved Tsutomu.

Michiko was unable to respond. Reflecting on her own emotions, she'd had a premonition that the time would come when her husband would ask her this question. Now, having actually heard the words from her husband's mouth, she thought that something terrible–something that ought not to exist in their life together–had occurred.

She felt that she shouldn't lie. She almost confessed, but something completely different came out of her mouth.

"Why do you say such a thing? That's terrible! I haven't the least…"

"I've been aware of what's going on for some time. Even if you haven't done anything, at least Tsutomu has some rather inappropriate feelings for you. Did he say something to you?"

"Is there any reason for him to say something?"

This was the truth, and the feeling of freedom that comes with telling the truth gave her the courage to speak out.

"Don't you think it's odd that he should leave the house so abruptly?" Akiyama said. "Even Tomiko was talking about his behavior."

"What did she say?"

Akiyama didn't respond. He thought he had put himself at a disadvantage. Not only was it unpleasant to have reported what Tomiko said, but he felt guilty having mentioned Tomiko at this moment.

"That's Tomiko's way," said Michiko. "Don't you know that by now? Do you believe her more than you believe me?"

"If you were believable, would I be asking?"

"If you can't trust me, then why are we living together? Trust me, and stop saying such things. I've never had feelings for Tsutomu or for anyone else."

Michiko surprised herself at how smoothly she was able to lie. Even so, she was keeping her fingers crossed this time, hoping her husband would believe her lie and that their marriage would not be destroyed. The only thing remaining between them was the outward form of husband and wife, but she had thought, out of custom, that a marriage was only a matter of outward appearances anyway.

Akiyama was shocked to hear Michiko so calmly deny something that should have been as clear to the two people in question as it was to him. For the first time ever he was afraid of his wife.

His fears were justified. She did not think she was acting at all badly toward Tsutomu by spitting out a denial of her love for him. Had she been asked before she'd observed Tsutomu's feelings, she might well have confessed. The fact that she lied, and felt at ease doing so, was because she was sure of Tsutomu's love. Although she valued the outward forms of marriage, she did not feel she should abandon Tsutomu. As long as she was content with being attuned to Tsutomu's heart, she had not considered what to do next.

"Really? I wonder…," Akiyama said after a short pause. "All right, then, so be it. But one way or the other, Tsutomu has to leave. You know very well that I've had to put up with all kinds of unpleasantness because he's here."

"We can't do that. Tsutomu's done nothing wrong. Think how Ōno will react."

"I'm aware of that." Akiyama was irritable again. "I can't stand relatives. You want to keep him in this house no matter what. I suppose it's all right, but can't we have him at least go away for a while? It's summer vacation, isn't it? There must be a friend's place somewhere."

· This plan left a number of thorny problems unresolved. He still didn't believe Michiko. He decided to pretend he believed her only because he, like his wife, nurtured the custom of respect for the outward forms of marriage. He just wanted to have his wife send her lover away for a while.

Michiko could hardly oppose him.

"I see," she said. "I suppose that's best, isn't it?"

The shadow of distress that skittered across her brow as she spoke gave Akiyama a perverse pleasure.

The deception lovers practice came naturally to Tsutomu, who was in a conflicted state of mind when he got back. He came in, smiling nonchalantly, but he couldn't help sense that something had happened between the two people facing each other on the veranda. For a long time Tsutomu recalled unpleasantly the momentary fear he detected in the ill-tempered face of Akiyama, who intentionally avoided looking at him.

Michiko turned to him with a welcoming expression, but there was none of the feeling he had expected to see in her eyes.

There is no need to go into any more detail about the remainder of that awkward day, or to record the anxiety Tsutomu experienced, especially during his time alone in the evening. Michiko's eyes had been lifeless, because it would not do to have both her husband and Tsutomu see through her heart. A man in love is not satisfied unless his lover's eyes are always filled with love—and when they are not, he is wretched.

Tsutomu's misfortune, however, was assuaged the next day when Akiyama purposely went out and Michiko spoke casually to him.

"Isn't there some place where you could go and have fun with your friends, now that Yuki-chan is on summer break?"

Michiko looked into Tsutomu's eyes for a long time. Tsutomu thought that he could detect love once more in her calm, contented expression.

"Did Akiyama say something?" he couldn't help but ask.

Michiko simply replied, "No," but her eyes told him different. She didn't say anything more, just continued to look into his eyes. He wanted to ask her all sorts of things, but he was afraid to shatter this pleasant, tacit conspiracy, and so he held his tongue.

A school friend who lived in Hayama had recently invited him to spend the summer, so he left.

He spent his holiday at the shore with several people, including his friend's older brother and younger sister. Separation added a new flavor to his love. Waves of happiness would wash over him at odd moments. His friend was really surprised by how quiet Tsutomu had become.

He took pleasure in turning over in his mind the meaning of the expression in Michiko's eyes. It definitely said that she loved him. At the same time it also told him, *Please don't make me unhappy*—which really meant, *Please don't tear me from my present peaceful state.* From the vantage of his youthful love, these two wishes were a contradiction. If her happiness required preserving that contradiction, then he would have to be patient.

Tsutomu often took solitary walks along the shore. On clear evenings he could see Mt. Fuji across Sagami Bay. It appeared taller and larger than when he viewed it from Hake. Commanding both the Tanzawa mountain range to its right, and a group of volcanoes that crossed from Hakone to Amagi on its left, it etched a sharp silhouette against the sunset glow of the sky. The volcanoes that erupted from the fault lines traversing the Japanese archipelago created elegant conical shapes because their craters did not shift position, but slowly continued to spew out lava and lapilli over long geological periods. Tsutomu had learned all this from a book in the elder Miyaji's library. If his love had that degree of patience and duration, he thought perhaps there might come at some point the means and opportunity to make his love a reality.

His friend's seventeen-year-old sister wore glasses. Once, as she ran up to him at the shore, a pouch fell out of her blouse. He thought it was cute the way she blushed as she picked it up out of the sand. If love were large-hearted in this fashion, it would spread over everything without focusing its light exclusively on a single object of desire.

Tsutomu's ever-present passion stirred in him the idea of visiting his mother. He hadn't seen her in years. She lived in Zushi with a younger man, a former diplomat for whom she had abandoned her family. Her new husband had lost his position as a result of his affair with Tsutomu's mother. After drifting from one job to another, he had finally become a cotton broker.

His job did not seem to be going all that well. He would invite his shifty-looking acquaintances from the black market to play mahjong at his house. Apparently that game was now his sole source of income.

In the presence of her husband, Tsutomu's mother was reserved in her display of affection for a child she had not seen in a long time. She was a different person from the spirited, colorful woman Tsutomu had known when he was a boy.

Seeing how his mother's difficult affair had turned out made Tsutomu shudder.

He became uneasy. Intoxicated by his own formless passion, having given no serious thought to the future of his love with Michiko, he now looked foolish to himself. It occurred to him that his unease would not subside until he saw Michiko. She had hinted when he left that he should be gone for two weeks. He came back to

Hake after a week.

Seeing the couple unexpectedly calm and on good terms, he felt betrayed. Michiko was as kind to him as always, but it irritated him that she was showering the same kindness on Akiyama.

He looked in vain for that expression in her eyes, which he had studied in his mind so much at Hayama. She merely smiled kindheartedly at him. Her love was contained entirely within her eyes, but that was not apparent to Tsutomu. Because he was uneasy, he was searching for the same unease in his partner.

Michiko's love had retreated a step. This was due to the progress of Tsutomu's love. Michiko was comfortable with this, because even though she herself had retreated, the distance between them had not changed. Thus it turned out that no matter how much Tsutomu moved toward her, she would withdraw an equal distance. In this way, when circumstances are difficult, a woman's love becomes unattainable to an extreme degree—provided of course that the woman does not make love a profession or a paranoid obsession.

Meanwhile, Akiyama had drawn a step closer to Michiko. After Tomiko pointed out to him the possibility that the logic he claimed for adultery was operating in his own home, he suddenly began to view the position and honor of a husband as extremely important. Consequently, he became less susceptible to Tomiko's charms.

He even thought that he really did love his wife after all. Michiko's virtues— her girlish kindness, her skill and modesty in running the household—had penetrated deep into his consciousness. Apart from all that, the habit of living together as husband and wife had taken on a new charm. He rarely went to Tomiko's house, and seemed to enjoy just being together with Michiko. On occasion he would even praise her cooking.

The behavior of a husband who has become conscious of his wife's virtues does not necessarily lead to all that much intimacy between a couple. What irritated Tsutomu is that Michiko had attuned herself to the change in her husband. Had he known her true feelings, he would not have been concerned. In fact, Michiko now considered Akiyama something of a nuisance.

Customs, in order to be customs, must remain implicit. As long as Michiko had feelings for Tsutomu, her relationship with Akiyama would remain precarious. That situation had not changed. However, there was the danger that Akiyama's artificial expressions of love would actually increase the risk to their relationship by exaggerating the customs of marriage. Only the fretfulness of the ignorant Tsutomu prevented a crisis from arising as a result of Akiyama's behavior.

Fretfulness spurred him on. It countered the impact on him of the unfortunate outcome of his mother's affair. He was inclined to pursue the difficulty of his love for the sake of its difficulty. *I won't be miserable like my mother*, he thought. He now wanted to snatch away the ever-calm Michiko's peace of mind. An expression came into his eyes that made Michiko afraid.

It became increasingly painful for this unhappy young man to live under the same roof with Michiko. He had time off from tutoring Yukiko, but he pretended there was homework during the summer break and regularly went over to Ōno's house. His visits grew longer.

More and more often he lingered after dinner, pulling a chair out onto the lawn and chatting with Ōno and Tomiko well into the evening.

Ōno didn't mind, in part because Tsutomu, like the subordinates at his company, listened quietly to his idle chatter. Ōno had decided that he would take Tsutomu into the company in the future, and so he naturally displayed the attitude of a guarantor. He liked the way Tsutomu quietly adapted to such a relationship.

Tsutomu actually listened with pleasure as Ōno talked about conditions in the soap factory, or detailed his problems with financing, which had recently become more pressing. Michiko was also planning for Tsutomu to go to work at Ōno's company, and she had discussed the matter with Tsutomu. Thus, it was pleasant for Tsutomu to listen to Ōno speaking, because it brought Michiko to mind.

As they gazed out at the peaceful scenery across the Nogawa basin, mist rising from the surface of the water obscured the lights in the distance. The calls of owls nesting in the grove at Hake awakened a yearning in Tsutomu. He wondered if Michiko wasn't talking pleasantly with Akiyama on the other side of that grove.

Bundles of searchlight beams from the neighboring airfield sent out parallel beacons that rose perpendicularly in the sky. As he looked at these lights, this veteran's heart was overcome with a surge of impatience he could not bear. Tsutomu thought, *Just how long must I obsess over this hopeless love?*

He felt the instinct to destroy all the relationships now suffocating him. If, in destroying those relationships, he gave birth to the same kind of chaos he had experienced on the battlefields of Burma, he thought he could survive. *These helpless dolls wouldn't know what to do under extreme conditions, but I'd be able to get along fine.*

He could sense that this fantasy was not practical, that he was powerless in the face of reality. Yet he simply could not suppress the fantasy, because the very desire not to suppress it was pleasurable.

The lawn was illuminated by outdoor lighting Ōno had installed. The lights were intended mainly to draw moths away, but they were also put in to keep out amorous couples from a nearby silk factory who were attracted to the spot. These couples would often huddle together in the darkness under the trees in the vicinity. They were always removing the bulbs from the streetlamps on the road below Hake, no matter how often the city replaced them.

Ōno installed his outdoor lighting in part for his own amusement. Ever since he was a boy, the son of a silk merchant, his idea of a joke was to irritate people by some sort of mischief.

People would sneak into the rear garden at Ōno's house. At one point they even broke down the fence. There were times when the sound of lovers singing in low voices mingled with their whispers.

Until very recently Tsutomu had indulged in that kind of sex. He had come to Hake precisely because he had grown weary of such affairs. Now he envied the freedom of those lovers.

Back then I wasn't trapped in a painful love, he thought. *Should I go back to the old crowd?* He was merely trying out idle thoughts—he was fully aware that, for now, he could not live apart from Michiko.

He began to feel attracted to Tomiko's coquettishness. Previously he had found her mannerisms tedious. Now that he was suffering because of the moral rectitude of a wife, Tomiko's flouting of convention and her dislike of her husband proved more agreeable.

Tomiko was always paying attention to Tsutomu, so she was sensitive to changes in his attitude. She knew very well why Akiyama had stopped coming over to perform his monologue on adultery. After all, she was the one who had warned him about Tsutomu. Michiko had become more important to Akiyama, while Tsutomu's position had become more difficult. This situation pleased Tomiko and encouraged her to draw closer to Tsutomu. A coquette acts according to circumstance, even as she is acted on by circumstance.

Although Tomiko felt something akin to love for Tsutomu, her desire did not go beyond drawing his heavy, youthful head to her breast. This was certainly not the kind of feeling Michiko could afford to have for Tsutomu. Yet that feeling was exactly what Tsutomu most wanted just now.

Truly Tomiko was one of a kind—a woman who could treasure his furtive glances, which expressed both youthful timidity and an unyielding spirit. These were looks that in fact he almost never gave to Michiko.

She did not choose the easy route of ridiculing Michiko to get closer to him. Such an approach would have been too trite for her, and in any case it would wound her pride to speak of her rival directly to Tsutomu. She sensed that there was something serious between him and Michiko that she did not understand, and that made her a little jealous. One evening her jealousy drove her to deliberately show off to Michiko just how close she was to Tsutomu.

It was a moonlit night. After Tsutomu had finished his usual routine with Yukiko, Ōno came home from the factory. The four of them were enjoying the cool air on the lawn when Akiyama and Michiko arrived in their summer robes. Ever since the day Akiyama mentioned what Tomiko had said about Tsutomu, Michiko had avoided meeting her unless it was absolutely necessary. This evening, however, she tagged along because she was concerned that Tsutomu was spending so much time lately at Tomiko's house.

The nearly full moon was hidden behind the trees on the slope for a while, but it gradually emerged and lit up the terrace. Stands of low trees, swollen with shadows, clumped together like islands on the fields below. The back gardens and the area beyond the hedge were occupied by couples from the factory, and their songs and laughter came drifting up to the terrace.

Ōno turned off the outside lighting. They had each brought out a rattan chair, and when Michiko and Akiyama arrived, Tsutomu was sitting with Yukiko between him and Tomiko. Tsutomu had been telling Yukiko the story of *Alice in Wonderland*. He was fond of this nine-year-old. She was special to him because he could always count on her to respond affectionately.

Akiyama and Ōno talked mainly about some articles in the newspaper. Having entertained hopes for Tomiko, Akiyama had grown to like Ōno. It flattered Akiyama's vanity to listen with disdain to Ōno's rambling stories.

Tomiko was especially kind to her daughter this evening. She held Yukiko's hand, stroked her hair, and explained various things about the children's story Tsutomu was narrating. She enjoyed demonstrating in front of her rival an affection she held in common with Tsutomu.

Tomiko's arrow struck home. Michiko felt like a fifth wheel sitting next to her. Her wariness regarding Tomiko's flirtations, which she had first experienced when she wasn't sure of her feelings for Tsutomu, came back to her.

She now began to regret the modesty with which she had laughingly responded to the look on Tsutomu's face, which, it seemed, had wanted to speak to her. It was almost as if she had been pushing him away.

She could not believe her eyes. Yukiko was holding hands with both Tomiko and Tsutomu. *Why was she holding them over her heart? In front of everyone in this bright moonlight? Could the two of them already be this intimate?*

Tomiko seemed to be looking at Tsutomu with a flirtatious smile. Tsutomu's face, darkened by the shadows cast by the moonlight, was apparently smiling back. *Could this really be happening?*

Jealousy had already reared up in Akiyama's chest. He was watching Tomiko's face. Her large eyes reflected the moonlight, and they glanced upward at him. He knew the meaning of that look. She was mocking him.

It soothed Akiyama's vanity to think that she was showing off her intimacy with Tsutomu in order to arouse him. And what he saw did succeed in stirring up a jealous reaction. Suddenly a new fear gripped him—would he have to spend his whole life feeling envious about everything?

Ōno continued to chatter away. At that moment he looked to Akiyama like the very epitome of all husbands—a true masterpiece.

Yukiko was sleepy, and went off to her bedroom. Tomiko followed after her. The murmur of their voices as they read a book could be heard from inside.

Tsutomu was silent. To Michiko he looked as though he were absorbed in listening to the voices. It was difficult to make herself share Tsutomu's interest.

"I wonder what they're reading?" Michiko murmured.

Tsutomu did not catch the drift of her question right away. He had not expected Michiko to start up a conversation. He wasn't really listening to Tomiko's voice, but instead was wondering why, in front of Michiko, he hadn't more quickly pulled back his hand, which had been clasped together with Yukiko's and Tomiko's. He'd actually had trouble extricating his hand, which had been tightly entwined with Tomiko's small, supple fingers.

He felt as if he were being dragged along hopelessly, even though he actually had very few expectations.

"A children's story, I think," he said. "I don't really know."

"Can't Yukiko read by herself?"

"She should be able to, I guess," Tsutomu half muttered to himself. "Tomiko seems to be doing something special tonight."

"She's always doing things on a whim," Ōno said, turning toward them. "I've never heard her read to Yukiko before."

"Tsutomu, could you come here? Yukiko has a question for you." Tomiko was calling from inside the house.

Tsutomu hesitated for a moment. He stood and Michiko looked up at him with a faint expression that caught his eyes. He stepped up on the veranda and entered the house.

Yukiko was already in bed. She was turned towards the wall. When he stepped across the threshold, Tomiko was standing in a corner just inside the door. She moved toward him, her whole body radiating a voluptuous charm. Tsutomu had only enough space to twist around and avoid her embrace. He bumped into something, and Yukiko, who was supposed to be asleep, cried out, "Mama, I don't want you to leave!" Her voice carried out into the garden. Michiko stood up.

Akiyama failed to notice his wife's movement, which might have served as a warning to him. He stood up as well, his attention drawn to the interior of the house.

Tsutomu came outside, a little out of breath. When Yukiko cried out, he startled himself by suddenly, violently pushing at Tomiko's chest. In a flash he recalled seeing the small figure of Yukiko lying with her face towards the wall.

Ōno brushed past Tsutomu as he entered the house. Yukiko's crying, mingled with the sound of her parents comforting her, drifted out to the garden. All that time Akiyama had been eyeing Tsutomu intently.

CHAPTER 7

THE LAKESHORE

Events that evening awakened a new resolve in Akiyama. He no longer suffered from constant jealousy. He believed he had to take some action in order to rid himself of his unpleasant emotions. Hadn't his mentor, Stendhal, exhorted both will and action? No one can tell where the fanaticism of this kind of epigone will lead.

He had more or less surmised that something had happened between Tsutomu and Tomiko that night in Yukiko's bedroom. It wasn't so much that he felt a great passion for Tomiko, but knowing that a woman he thought he loved had been rejected aroused his masculine vanity. That rejection caused him to overlook for a moment his concerns about the infidelity of his wife and his own husbandly honor.

He started to drop by Tomiko's house more frequently. After the incident, Tsutomu would no longer hang around the place, so Akiyama faithfully replaced him.

Akiyama had never seen Tomiko so weak. He gazed in distress at the weary, melancholy way she answered him, and the way her words were somehow twisted by her solitary thoughts. He thought he understood what she was going through.

Tomiko seemed lost in her thoughts. These days Ōno was often away on business. Sales of his soap had fallen badly, and in order to cut costs he had to procure cheaper raw materials. He went more frequently to the Kyoto-Osaka region in order to haggle with the brokers there, and often returned in a foul mood. The household budget was as lavish as ever, but Tomiko clearly understood that eventually their extravagant lifestyle would become impossible to maintain. When Ōno was away she would lie down and take a nap near a window facing the rear garden, where the sounds of the large brown cicada seethed. She would dream of Tsutomu entering, then wake up. She had never before been rejected by a man.

Everyone there that evening assumed Tsutomu left because Yukiko cried out. In fact Tomiko realized that he had rejected her even before Yukiko woke up.

Her technique of hiding in a corner of a room or hallway and then suddenly throwing herself at a man had worked without fail on her husband's acquaintances. But as soon as he saw her, Tsutomu put his hands out in front of him. After the way they had been holding hands in the garden, his reaction was not at all what she anticipated.

She could still vividly see the look of fear in Tsutomu's face. She never imagined she would see such an expression on him.

She thought she glimpsed in his heart a thorough preoccupation with someone else—that is, she saw that he was in love with Michiko.

And she was right. When she called Tsutomu into the house, he had pretty much guessed what she was up to. The feelings he experienced when they had been holding hands in the garden had lingered, and he was thinking about the pleasure of being led on that way. Thus he responded purely instinctively when he raised his hands to push her away.

He now recognized how firm his love was, and that made him even more miserable. He still could not bring himself to speak to Michiko, even though it wouldn't have been wrong for him to do so.

Michiko did not realize that Tsutomu had rejected Tomiko, so all she could do was worry about what she saw as their dangerous relationship. It was truly hard for her to determine, in her heart, whether or not she was jealous. In any case, she persuaded herself that everything she felt was for Tsutomu's sake. For an ethical spirit such as hers, even emotions are tinged by morality.

She tormented herself, wondering if it wasn't her own self-restraint that had pushed Tsutomu toward a relationship with Tomiko. This torment in no way lessened her support for him—she remained deeply concerned about Tsutomu's future, since he continued to rely on Ōno's assistance.

If her feelings were hypocritical, then it must be acknowledged that most moral sentiments are hypocritical.

One day, when Akiyama had gone over to visit Tomiko's house, Michiko at last broached the subject to Tsutomu.

"You haven't been eating dinner much at Ōno's lately," she said. "Is something wrong?"

"Not really, I just don't eat there. No particular reason."

"Oh, all right then. I was just thinking that maybe something happened."

Tsutomu blushed, and Michiko thought, *Just as I suspected.* His reaction gave her the courage to say what was on her mind.

"The other night you and Tomiko were acting rather strange and, well...I'm very concerned about you two. Even if nothing like that had happened before...there are times I can't sleep at night thinking it might have been my fault."

These were the first words hinting at love that Tsutomu had ever heard from Michiko. Tears came to his eyes. They looked at each other for a few moments without saying anything.

"You ought to know how I feel, Mit-chan," he said. "It's cruel of you to have such ideas. Why would I do anything with a woman like her?"

Michiko let out a sigh.

"Why do you always avoid me like that, Mit-chan?" Tsutomu took her hand as he spoke. She nervously tried to pull away, but in the end let him hold her hand.

Michiko thought that she must stoutly refuse him, but at the same time she could barely resist the urge to do the same thing Tomiko had wanted to do.

Tsutomu wanted to embrace Michiko, but he was put off by the fear in her eyes. So he took the liberty of putting all his passion into grasping her hand. He felt he must tell her everything he had repeated in his heart so many times.

"Can we ever be together?"

"What are you talking about?" Michiko smiled. "I'm just a housewife. After all I'm..."

The words "married to Akiyama" stuck in her throat. To actually speak those words would have been altogether too miserable for both Tsutomu and herself. All the joyless details of her life with Akiyama came to mind, and she started to cry.

"You don't need to worry about Akiyama," said Tsutomu. "Just the other day, the guy was going on and on at Tomiko's house about how irrational marriage is."

Michiko found the word "guy" objectionable.

"He was just playing up to Tomiko," said Michiko. "I'm the one who's at fault here. This won't do."

"In my experience all husbands are despicable."

"Don't say that! Such a dangerous way of thinking! You really are depraved, aren't you?"

"Depraved or not, does it really matter?"

"You should be ashamed. And you need to wise up. Until the world says depravity doesn't matter, you'd better not be showing it off."

This Machiavellian touch in Michiko's outlook surprised Tsutomu. Then again, she was simply mouthing the phrases her father had used on her oldest brother, the wandering poet: "You mustn't publish your poetry until society is ready to praise it."

They continued to talk, but her heart was hardening, and the young man was becoming self-centered. Their conversation started to repeat itself, so there's no need to record it all here.

At that very moment Akiyama and Tomiko were engaged in a conversation of a different sort. Akiyama was trying to convince Tomiko that it was foolish of her to be enamored of Tsutomu.

"A young man like that could never appreciate your good points," Akiyama said.

His desire for Tomiko had turned serious, and the presence of a rival, Tsutomu, transformed his interest in taking her away from Ōno into something of an obsession. True to form for Akiyama, he thought he would be able to win her heart through persuasion.

"I can't understand why you're so fond of him," he said. "You shouldn't be offended just because the boy turned away. You know he's in love with Michiko. A woman like her is just right for a sentimental youth."

Tomiko was a little surprised to hear him speak so nonchalantly. After all, this was the man who had rushed headlong back home when he heard her say that Michiko and Tsutomu were "just right" for each other.

"It's not right to speak that way about your wife," she said. "If Ōno said things like that about me, I'd hate him."

"Ōno wouldn't speak that way because he doesn't have someone he's in love with like I do."

"And who would that be?"

"You."

"You're very clever, aren't you? But I've heard that from a lot of men, so it doesn't affect me."

"That's because there hasn't been a man who's as sincere as I am."

"I doubt that."

"I've abandoned Michiko."

"Don't be stupid. I mention Tsutomu one time and you go pale and scamper back home."

"Have I ever really done that?"

Akiyama was feigning amnesia. He thought that Tomiko had come a long way toward him.

"You're sure Michiko wouldn't go that far with Tsutomu?" Tomiko asked.

She had hit her mark.

"He wouldn't go that far with you, would he?"

Tomiko grew haughty.

"Stop it. I've never even thought about that."

Desire overcame Akiyama, and he came up with a high-minded strategy not at all like him—that is, he hit upon the idea of praising his opponent.

"Tsutomu has a peculiar attractiveness that makes even men admire him," he said. "He's like a spirit, because you can never quite catch hold of him."

Tomiko had heard him use the word "spirit" on many occasions. He had borrowed the word from some foreign study of Stendhal's heroes, and she was fond of it because it so perfectly suited the elusive quality of the attraction she felt for Tsutomu. Simultaneously, she felt inclined to revise her view of Akiyama, who had spoken the word. At the very least, he had said something witty and smart.

Her expression of good will allowed him to make a proposition that struck even Akiyama as bold. He suggested that they go off somewhere and relax the next time Ōno went on a business trip. Ōno had already made plans to travel to the Kyoto-Osaka region to obtain a large order of whale oil from a merchant there. Akiyama knew that Ōno had promised to take Yukiko sightseeing with him.

If possible, Akiyama wanted to go with Tomiko and spend the night together somewhere. Lovers in the foreign novels he read often strolled along the shores of lakes. He had a little money from his translations hidden away from his wife, and he wanted to imitate those fictional lovers. He set his sights on one of the five lakes near Mt. Fuji, which they could get to quickly by way of the Chūō line.

Tomiko was caught off guard by the audacity of this college professor. She laughed and did not reply. As it happens, his proposition had also occurred to her. The difference was that, in her plan, Tsutomu was her partner.

At some point, after he had begun going over to Tomiko's house on a regular basis, Tsutomu had mentioned his interest in topography to her. He was particularly interested in the heights at Sayama, which had been the delta of the ancient Tamaga-wa. The heights now stood isolated, rising in the center of the Musashino plain. He wanted to go there at least once.

The Murayama Reservoir, which supplied water to metropolitan Tokyo, was surrounded by the hilly terrain of Sayama. The reservoir had been completed when Tomiko was a student, and the view of the manmade lake that filled the valley drew the citizens of Tokyo—especially student couples. Tomiko knew of the so-called "lovers' rest" hotels that lined the lakeshore. She thought she could take advantage of his interest in topography to invite him there. She too had some money stashed away that she kept secret from her husband.

Having been rejected by him once, Tomiko made a considerable sacrifice of her self-respect when she mentioned her idea to Tsutomu. Her invitation was flatly rejected. Not only did his face reveal a frigid indifference, but he admonished her in a manner inappropriate to his age. She had already decided not to go with Ōno on his trip, so Tsutomu's refusal drove her, out of desperation, to accept Akiyama's proposition. She had been bored ever since the death of her lover.

August was coming to an end. The plan was to tell everyone that Akiyama was going to his hometown in Saitama prefecture, and that Tomiko was going to visit a friend in Ōiso. They would stay over two nights.

They met at Tachikawa station and boarded a crowded train on the Chūō line. This was Akiyama's first trip with a woman since he had taken Michiko to Yuga-wara on their honeymoon. He was puffed up with joy that he was finally going on a trip with the woman he coveted; but as they were being jostled about in the car by black-market peddlers and young gang members, he began to feel miserable. No matter how clever he had been in persuading her to come, it was clear he had only a secondary place in her heart.

Tomiko was distracted as well. Her lingering dissatisfaction at having been rejected by Tsutomu made her regret the careless decision to go on this trip with Akiyama. Even after they managed to get seats when the train passed Yose, they only gazed silently at the scenery of the narrow valleys of the Katsuragawa gliding past their window.

They transferred to an electric train at Ōtsuki. It too was packed. Most Japanese at the time had yet to resume the custom of taking a summer retreat, so excursion trains like this one were filled at the end of summer with people carrying all kinds of food. Even here the thirty-year-old and forty-year-old lovers felt oddly restrained and did not speak to one another.

The train rumbled along as it made its way up the Katsuragawa. Akiyama searched for Mt. Fuji. He was not particularly enamored of the scenery, but his choice of this locale was motivated by a corrupt desire. He could see Mt. Fuji from here, and since Fuji could be seen from Hake, he could indirectly parade his infidelity before the people of Hake.

Fuji was obscured by the low mountains bordering the river and was not clearly visible. Just as Akiyama had tired of waiting for it, suddenly it came into view. This wasn't the compact shape he viewed from Hake. A sternly dignified mountain, crowned with the rust color of volcanic stone, towered above the window. Akiyama found it hard to breathe.

Some of the lava that formed the base of Mt. Fuji was exposed at the lakeside at Kawaguchi, and desolate rock formations in the garden of their inn were embedded in the earth or split into pillars that tilted toward the surface of the lake. The shallow waters spreading out before those rock formations were muddy, like the color of water in a gutter.

The maid sat in their room for a few moments sizing up the couple.

She told them, "Please feel free to use the bath together," but the shy Akiyama found it difficult to take advantage of the maid's words to invite Tomiko to go with him. Alone in the deserted tile bath, he once again felt wretched as he hurriedly washed his body.

Tomiko came into the bath after him. She wore a padded robe. She smiled, seeing him there. She had finally begun to take compassion on him, finding him forlorn.

At dinner Akiyama forced himself to drink beer, which he normally couldn't stand. Tomiko wasn't the kind of woman who drank if the man wasn't drinking, but on this occasion she got even more drunk than Akiyama. A popular recording was playing over a loudspeaker in a pavilion on a nearby promontory. It set off a raucous reverberation on the surface of the lake. The two of them had nothing at all to talk about.

That night, for the first time in his life, Akiyama had sex with a woman other than his wife. The experience did not bring him the pleasure he had privately dreamed of—that empty space he always sensed between his body and his wife's body was there between Tomiko and him as well.

They slept in separate bedding, their backs to one another. He was surprised by the thirst he continued to feel in his heart. For the first time he had real doubts, wondering if the things he desired were nothing more than illusions.

Tomiko's thoughts were more or less the same. Akiyama's caresses, like those of all the men she had loved other than her husband, were filled with a trivial sentimentality. She was a woman whose sensitivity compelled her to feel disgust and pleasure simultaneously. She believed that all men were performers, playacting their roles.

She dreamed that there was no actor in Tsutomu. Perhaps she would be saved if only she could imagine that giving her body to a man she didn't really love was a dream.

When she turned her back to Akiyama and closed her eyes, she also felt a thirst.

Arising the next morning, Akiyama noticed that Tomiko quickly pulled on her tabi.

The sky was overcast. Mt. Fuji was wreathed in deep clouds. Evergreen trees swept down the trace of one of the newer lava flows. The wildly overgrown base of the mountain spread before them, filling their field of vision. The lobby of the inn was deserted. Lava stalactites and the specimens of butterflies that lived in the fields skirting the foot of Mt. Fuji were covered in dust. The swallowtail butterfly of Fuji resembled the butterflies he had watched with Michiko and Tsutomu that day in the garden at Hake.

Utterly bored, they took a boat out onto the lake. An automobile motor had been attached to a flat wooden boat of traditional design. It wasn't very fast, and they proceeded at a monotonous pace across the dark green water, heading for a small island in an arm of the lake. They passed a rock jutting out of the water, and the boatman abandoned his steering, came over to them, and told them of the legend of a maid who went to and from her lover by swimming between that rock and the island. Both Akiyama and Tomiko sensed that they were being mocked.

When they passed the island, the arm of the lake narrowed and was squeezed between the low mountains of the ancient Misaka stratum, which had been formed by a lava flow from Mt. Fuji. The view of the utterly nondescript forest there, which contrasted with the plains at the foot of the mountain, somehow made them feel more at ease.

A dull shaft of light seeped from the clouds, illuminating one of the mountains on their way. The mountain was deeply eroded, and its steep incline slid precipitously down to the edge of the lake. There were no houses, and the place made them both feel lonely, as if they were moving on the periphery of human life.

As they came round the island on their way back, clouds rolled down from Mt. Fuji, flying at full tilt toward the lake. It started to rain.

They decided to cut short their plans to return to the inn and tried to go home, but the torrential rain stopped them. The radio reported that a typhoon, which had started near Iōjima off the coast of Kyushu, had suddenly gathered force from Hachijōjima off the Izu peninsula. It made landfall at Odawara and was moving toward Usui in Gumma prefecture. It was too much to return home through such a storm, and so they stayed on another night.

All through the evening they could hear the wind rasping over the surface of the lake and mingling with the tapping of the rain on the eaves. They couldn't sleep. There was tenderness in Tomiko's lovemaking that night.

CHAPTER 8

SAYAMA

At the same moment Akiyama and Tomiko were together, another couple was at a different hotel in a different location. Tsutomu and Michiko had also been caught in the storm and had to stay at one of the hotels along the shore of the Murayama Reservoir, which is tucked away in the heights at Sayama.

The storm was blowing fiercely. A typhoon named Catherine was cutting across the Sagami plain, passing through the gap between the Sayama heights and the mountainous region of Kantō as it headed toward the Tōhoku region.

Tomiko's invitation to go for a stroll at Sayama had given Tsutomu the idea of inviting Michiko. She had agreed to this slightly risky proposal only because her husband's absence gave her the freedom to do so. They went out the day after Akiyama and Tomiko left. Because Ōno and Yukiko had already left for their trip to the Kyoto-Osaka region, no one was at Hake on this particular day.

It had been overcast since morning. The newspapers had reported the approach of the typhoon, but its initial forecast was for a track that would move north by northwest, with the storm making landfall on the Atsumi peninsula. Red iron warning signs had been posted at the train stations, but once the two had taken the trouble to come this far, they didn't feel like going back home.

The Tamako line, which headed toward Sayama from Kokubunji, traveled through woods dotted with the red roofs of schools and buildings peeking up through pines and trees. The train came to a halt, and the screech of cicada grew louder in the stand of trees around the station. This chorus of insects, which could be heard singing in all the trees all over Musashino, called to mind expansive fields filled with cicada voices.

When the train pulled out of Kokubunji station, a feeling of calm release filled Michiko's heart. It had been so long since she had gone out with Tsutomu like this; because of the present strains upon their relationship, this excursion was unexpected. However, when the chance came for them to actually go on this little trip, she felt as though it was perfectly natural. She also felt as though she had just been liber-

73

ated. Where would this condition lead her? Her feeling of relief was so great, and her affection had been so painful until now, that she had had no time to ponder such a question.

The forests eventually thinned and open fields came into view. Mulberry trees and rows of tea shrubs served as partitions for dry rice paddies and vegetable patches growing bountifully. Farmhouses dotted the landscape, surrounded by trees that served as windbreaks. In the distance something that looked like a tank raised its ominous shape high above the flat fields.

The gentle, rolling fields of Musashino appeared to be rising toward Sayama. The train continued forward without pause, though they could sense in the sound of the engine a slight straining as they moved up the incline. A line of hills, linked like some folding screen, came into view before them.

Tsutomu had consulted some books in Miyaji's collection before setting off. He learned that the heights at Sayama were located southwest of Tokorozawa, about thirty kilometers west of Tokyo. They straddled metropolitan Tokyo and Saitama prefecture, forming an oval approximately thirty kilometers in circumference and about one hundred and fifty meters above sea level. The heights at Sayama stood apart on the Musashino plateau like an earthen rampart and were level with the heights on the opposite bank of the Tamagawa, ten kilometers to the south.

The heights at Sayama were originally the delta of the ancient Tamagawa. This river had at one time flowed out from Ōme into the sea bed of Tokyo Bay, which back then had penetrated as far as the eastern edge of the Kantō mountain range. It had deposited a yellow-brown sediment of sand and pebbles, which is now called the Itsukaichi stratum because it is exposed at a spot near present-day Itsukaichi City. After a succession of upheavals and subsidings, the entire land mass that was the original delta came to tower above the Musashino plateau. The heights faced the sea on the eastern side. They were deeply eroded, and two valleys had developed in the center. Water and sewer engineers from Tokyo blocked up these valleys at the end of the Meiji Period in order to store the waters of the Tamagawa that flowed from Ōme. In doing so, they unintentionally reconstructed the channel of the ancient Tamagawa.

The Murayama Reservoir swallowed up the southern valley, and in the late 1920s it became popular in the cultural circles of Ginza as a convenient place for excursions. The hotels that went up along the lake shore were built in response to demand from these outings. These strange buildings, with their eclectic mix of Western and Japanese architectural elements, fell into disuse during the war and became dilapidated. Children on school trips were now just about the only guests who enlivened the shoreline, but usually they did not stay for the night. Tsutomu, who had wanted to visit Sayama out of his curiosity about the topography of the area, knew nothing about these hotels.

When the train stopped at the final station on the line, Sayama Park, they could see a green-gray dam blocking the way about fifteen meters above them. Dwarf pines grew below the embankment in a modern-style park with twisting paths running through the lawns. Tsutomu felt strangely ticklish as he led Michiko through this city-planned garden. They climbed zigzag steps at the spot where the dam ended.

The reservoir was full there.

The still waters, which were about twenty-five meters deep, reflected the edge of the low bank that descended from the crown of the hill, spreading out in a green tint. A water intake tower with an oddly snug, rounded roof, jutted out into the water. At the approach to the dam there was a Western-style building, which looked like some kind of office. It had apparently been a military assembly post, for it bore a sign that read "No Entry."

Tsutomu glanced back. This was more or less the center of the valley on the south side of the heights, and his field of vision was blocked by the ridgeline that extended on both sides. Rolling hillocks and woods nearly covered the roofs of houses and temples at the exit of the valley. Their undulations made the dark greens of late summer seem stagnant under the overcast sky.

Tsutomu expected the heights at Sayama to provide an observation platform that commanded a view of Musashino, which spread out below them in the shape of a fan. But the heights are a mere fifty meters taller than the surrounding area of Musashino, which itself is about eighty meters above sea level, so the line of sight was obstructed by a small rise that led up to the heights from the east.

Tsutomu thought that if he walked out onto one of the headlands of the heights he could perhaps get a better view, but since Michiko was accompanying him he decided against it. In any case it is natural for lovers to prefer the water, and so he and Michiko decided to head to the left to circle the man-made lake.

They walked a short distance beneath a row of cherry trees that had been planted in strict accordance to the aesthetics of urban planning. The path followed the ridgeline and then turned off to their right. The reddish soil descended toward the lake, between red pines, right down to the surface of the water. Evening primrose dotted the slope with a fragile green, creating the impression that they had been placed there by the same urban planner who put in the cherry trees. They caught glimpses along the way of a path meandering farther below. Entrance to that path was prohibited, perhaps to protect the purity of the water. For lovers who prefer the water, this prohibition was an act of betrayal.

A ruined teahouse was boarded up beside the path. No one else was there. Their surroundings were perfectly still.

Tsutomu was happy. He had not been on a leisurely walk alone with Michiko since the time they had hiked upstream along the Nogawa, which was before they had recognized that they were in love.

Tsutomu felt impelled to remind Michiko of that time, and she recalled the moment at Koigakubo when she first identified her feelings for Tsutomu as love. That was not even two months ago, but she felt that a great deal had changed. If she had changed, had her life back then been a complete lie, and her present life the truth? Or was her present suffering a lie, and her former life the truth?

While Michiko was interrogating herself, Tsutomu became intoxicated by his happiness. He sensed that her unreserved kindness of old would return because they were walking along together like this. Why must they feel compelled to identify their feelings as love?

The path they were walking created the impression from time to time that they were far away from the water, but then he realized that the path was built to follow the lake, which penetrated the hills to a surprisingly deep extent. Because the reservoir was located in the heart of the Sayama heights, it was hemmed in by the capricious contours of the surrounding hillsides, which had not been worn away naturally. The water of the lake had not had time to alter the character of the loam on the shore, and its burnt sienna color slanted right into the edge of the water.

On the outer side of the hill was a similar valley that had been eroded deeply. It was filled with old paddies, tea fields, and thatched roofs. People had inhabited this outer side, which formed the southern face of the hill, since ancient times. Now tea was cultivated on those warm slopes.

This spot commanded a view of Musashino as well. The green plain spread out in the distance, and they could see as far as the woods at Hake, and beyond to the heights of Tama in the distance. Cirrus clouds, harbingers of a storm, towered darkly in the sky. A gust of wind came along, as if it had just remembered something, swaying the roadside pampas grass that had just come into its flowery tufts.

"Is it going to rain?"

Michiko looked up as she spoke. A low-flying twin-engine craft, its silver wings shining dully, was slowly descending beneath the low clouds and heading for an airstrip nearby.

"Don't worry. If it starts to rain, we can head back." Tsutomu smiled.

An old man in a uniform, perhaps the superintendent of the reservoir, came walking slowly up to them. He passed by, looking amazed that a couple should be strolling along so nonchalantly in this kind of weather. When he disappeared around a curve on the path, Tsutomu suddenly said, "We'd better go in," and headed for a stand of trees leading down to the lake where there was a sign that read, "No Entry."

"Won't he get mad at us?" said Michiko.

"The old man just came this way, so it's safe." Tsutomu laughed, displaying his soldierly cunning.

The woods, a mix of various trees amid the red pines, sloped gently down to the lakeshore. Tsutomu intended to walk as far as the shore and then go along a narrow side path. But soon they stepped onto a promontory that jutted out into the lake.

He noticed that the erosion of the banks on both sides was unexpectedly deep. The promontory looked as if it had been squeezed up to the point where the land began to be covered by the forest.

Near the shore at the tip of the promontory, they sat down amid the wildly blooming evening primrose. The water was all around them, and ripples on the surface of the lake raced right, then left, following the change in the wind.

Tsutomu put his arm around Michiko's shoulder. They kissed each other, without calculation, as though it had all been decided in advance.

Tsutomu tasted something in Michiko's lips that he knew from long ago. It was a taste he had experienced sometime in the distant past. It resembled the scent of his young mother's breast when he was a small child.

Michiko caught a scent about Tsutomu. It was the smell of something dark she had sensed in him after he had been repatriated. It startled her. She opened her eyes and pulled her body away.

But the face she saw was that of her beloved cousin. It was the face of the quiet youth of old. She was confused.

Their second kiss was much longer. Michiko felt more distressed. Before they kissed, her upper lip was twisted slightly, like the mouth of a child who has just tasted something sour. While they kissed, Tsutomu found picturing that expression pleasurable.

They said nothing. Tsutomu's lips did not force themselves on her, and that made Michiko feel more at ease. She thought, *If this is love, then loving Tsutomu is not wrong. If we followed from the intimacy of our childhood a path that leads us of its own accord to love, then so be it. Even so, wouldn't it be best not to kiss him again?* She would always remember this sweetness, which she was tasting for the first time in her life.

The wind began to rustle the treetops. At some point the surface of the lake had been overspread with triangular waves. The gusts of wind seemed to move across the center of the lake as if to smooth out these whitecaps.

Rain struck their cheeks. They stood up and made their way back to the path. Musashino was already misty, and sluggish clouds covered the sky. By the time they crossed the second dam that divided the center of the reservoir, they were being buffeted by sustained winds.

The water level on the upper reservoir was about six meters higher than that of the lower reservoir. In the interior recesses of the reservoir a hilltop formed the western side that closed off the lake. Beyond that the mountains of the Kantō range were covered in clouds, occasionally peeking through like a woman shaking out her disheveled hair. White mist rose from where the water fell into the lower reservoir at the edge of the weir; gusts of wind swept the mist aside from time to time.

A thick driving rain suddenly assaulted them. They hurried across the dam, and ran into a teahouse at the other end.

A young man in army surplus clothing was hurriedly putting up rain shutters. As he did so, the earthen floor darkened beneath a dirty bare table. The rain clattered noisily on the zinc roof. As a courtesy, they ordered a soda. Tsutomu was smiling as they sipped it. He remained happy. The rain and the storm were a joy to him.

Michiko asked, "Are we going to be all right? It's really raining out there."

"I don't know. It's no big deal, just the remnants of the typhoon. Let's borrow an umbrella and we'll be fine."

Michiko was uneasy. It was already three o'clock. If these were the aftereffects of the typhoon, then the rain and wind would be really severe. *Would the house be all right? Had the old woman she asked to look after it while they were out properly closed the doors and windows? If the storm got worse and they couldn't get back, what would happen? What would Akiyama say?*

Michiko couldn't stand for Tsutomu to be so calmly drinking the soda. Because she had to keep her mind on household matters, even at a time like this, she began to feel miserable.

Hoping the rain would end was mere wishful thinking on Michiko's part. It fell more and more intensely, like any typical windstorm. The young man in the teahouse obviously wanted to close up shop at once and go home in the village below. He urged them to go to the hotel beside the first dam.

It turned out that they had only been waiting for the rain and wind to get worse. They asked if they could buy the young man's old, beat-up umbrella, and went out into the rain. The wind quickly ripped the umbrella to shreds. The path that followed the ridgeline was similar to the one on the opposite bank. It was washed out in places and rocks had tumbled down. Trees had been removed on the outer slope, exposing the ground, and the evening primrose had been flattened by a mudslide of reddish soil. The field and paddies were obscured in the rain, which was coming down at a slant. The surface of the lake was hazy.

They were soaked to the skin, so they hurried on as fast as they could. Turning bend after bend in the path, they felt discouraged, wondering, *Aren't we there yet?* At last they reached a point where they could see the hotel.

The hotel's lawn stretched all the way down to the lakeshore. It was shabby and tumbledown. The dimly lit lobby contained only a few cheap tables and chairs lined up like some low-class diner. Everything was dusty and dank.

They found out that the typhoon had suddenly changed course and made landfall at Odawara. It was now bearing down on the heights of Sayama. An accident in the electric grid cut service on the Tamako line, which they needed to get back home.

They had no time to think about anything. And they would not feel like humans again until they had shed their wet clothes. They changed into shabby, lattice-striped summer robes, then went to take a bath.

The sole embellishment in their room was a big double bed. Two cheap chairs had been placed there purely for show. Confronted with those chairs, Michiko realized that the situation was becoming serious. The concern she felt back at the teahouse had become a reality. In her heart she murmured, *What should I do? What should I do?* It was clear that, no matter what, they would have to stay the night. She had a premonition that at some point something terrible would happen between Tsutomu and her.

She had few options other than to observe Tsutomu closely. Her eyes seemed to devour him. The fearless smile had disappeared from his face. He stared intently at the raindrops outside the window, lost deep in thought.

The electricity was out, so they were told they would have to eat while it was still light. They had an awful meal in the dining hall at five o'clock. The only other guests were a foreign couple and their companions. Otherwise, the dining hall was deserted. One of the foreigners was whistling, apparently amused by the storm. The rain continued to get worse and worse, and water trickled down the walls on both sides of the windows. The surface of the lake, visible from the windows, was now a white haze. The triangular wave tops were blown about, and twilight had settled in.

They said little, and only spoke ramblingly about whether or not the trains would run the next day, or whether or not the house was all right—things they could do nothing about no matter how much they fretted.

That evening a small oil lamp was brought to their room.

"Tsutomu? Shall we just stay up all night?" Michiko was sitting in one of the chairs. Tsutomu nodded. They were in love, but face-to-face in that room they did nothing more than what they had done earlier by the lake.

"What will happen to us?" she said. "Will Akiyama forgive us for staying here tonight?"

"Don't worry. We haven't done anything to feel guilty about."

"Yes, but people won't think that way. Especially my husband."

"I shouldn't have asked you to come along."

"It's not your fault. I wanted to come with you."

"If we just stand firm, it won't matter what people say."

The lamp began to give out. They kissed—a kiss that seemed endless. Tsutomu could not control his desire. Michiko, in his embrace, softly called out, "Please don't." She moved her hands away, but soon they were once again entwined around Tsutomu's neck, and she was merely mouthing the words, "Please don't, please don't," over and over. Even as she resisted Tsutomu, her body was opening up in response to his strength, as though she begrudged ever letting go of him.

This was the moment Tsutomu had been waiting for. Then he heard a noise outside the window.

There was a thump that sounded as if something would break the outer structure of the building. This was followed by a long, piercing noise like a human voice—a sustained, thin, reverberating wail that penetrated the chaotic sounds of the storm outside.

Tsutomu glanced at Michiko.

He thought the noise was the crying voice of Michiko's spirit, which was now crumbling before him.

That spirit seemed to tell him, "Please don't, it's not right." The voice within his own heart told him, "Don't do this." If Michiko did not want to make love with him, it would not do to force himself on her.

Tsutomu pulled Michiko's hands away from his neck, and placed them on her breast. Michiko's head, like a child saying no, swayed slightly left and right. Her closed eyes looked like wounds on her anguished face.

Michiko was aware at once that there was a space between their bodies, and she opened her eyes. Tsutomu smiled. Joy suddenly flashed across her face, expressing both her anxiety and surprise. She embraced Tsutomu's neck again.

"You're wonderful, Tsutomu. You're a good man after all." She covered his face with kisses.

Tsutomu didn't know which was better—having sacrificed himself, or experiencing the joy of such kisses.

They stayed up all night, sitting next to each other in the darkness until morning. Tsutomu kept listening intently to the wailing that continued to reverberate outside. Michiko, for her part, listened only to Tsutomu's occasional loud sighs.

CHAPTER 9

SEPARATION

The Tamako line had not restored service by the following morning, so they started the trip home on foot. Downed tree limbs and broken pieces of zinc roofing were scattered everywhere, blocking the red clay road, which was washed out here and there by the storm. Smoke rising straight up from a chimney in the distance across the paddies and fields showed that the wind was calm after the storm. The top of the plume of smoke slowly spread out like a fan, mingling with some wispy clouds that remained in the sky.

Water flowed swiftly through the ditches along the road. Some people had risen early and were clearing away the debris clogging a ditch in front of a house that looked like a country store.

It takes time to walk the distance a train can travel in fifteen minutes. Not having slept all night, they grew weary on the road that ran parallel to the rail line, where the houses were scattered more than three hundred meters apart. They walked in silence.

Although the storm had left them with no choice, it slowly dawned on Tsutomu that there was no undoing the fact that they had spent the night together. Akiyama would probably not forgive them, and Tsutomu would have to leave Hake, even though he had done nothing to deserve exile.

The restraint he had exercised the night before, when he was just a step short of achieving what probably would have been his supreme happiness, was very strange. Considering the nature of the feelings between Michiko and him, he really thought that sex with her was inappropriate. Yet since embracing her had been such a natural thing for him to do, why, when Michiko barely resisted him, had he thought it wouldn't be right to have sex?

Hearing the wail of the storm outside the window as the crying of Michiko's soul was of course an illusion; but if there had been nothing in his heart to lead him to think so, then he would never have heard the crying. It is a rather poignant truth that the hearts of people in love communicate to each other.

His premonition that he would be forced to leave Hake now made him regret his good conduct. He thought, *That's right. I have to undo this mistake. I'll have to stick it out at Hake, even if Akiyama says something.* Tsutomu was unaware that his eyes were flashing viciously.

Michiko was afraid. Thinking about how she had almost yielded to Tsutomu, she knew that because of what had happened last night her love, which had been her pride and pleasure amidst all the distress, was finished. Reflecting further on the workings of her heart, which simultaneously rejoiced at and regretted Tsutomu's self-control, she was even more convinced that her love was over. All through the night until dawn, each time Tsutomu sighed heavily, she would compare those sighs to her own frightened, expectant heart. From now on she must avoid living under the same roof with her cousin. She thought it sad that she had to fear the body walking beside her.

As they neared Kokubunji station the houses became more numerous, and the sight of people busily cleaning up after the storm eased Michiko's heart. Worried that her house had been damaged, she wanted to get home quickly and take care of things. She hurried Tsutomu, who continued to walk along lost in his thoughts.

When they finally arrived, a little past ten o'clock, the old lady who had been house-sitting for them glared and complained. She was worried about her own place, but had had to stay here because they hadn't shown up. She left right away. The old house had suffered some damaged. The wisteria arbor had collapsed and was beyond repair. Tsutomu placed his hand on Michiko's shoulder and she covered it with hers, then gently removed it. He patched the two low fences on both sides of the gate. His only comfort was that Michiko's hand was slightly fearful. Her face was smiling as always.

"Let it be for now," she said. "Let's get some sleep." Under the roof of the old house at Hake, those words could only mean, "Let's go to our own rooms." Tsutomu's face was tense.

They went to their rooms and each took a brief nap. Akiyama returned presently. He was in an excellent mood. He called together some workmen from the neighborhood and expertly cleared the place. Michiko immediately told him that she and Tsutomu had spent the previous evening at Murayama. She did that right away so that it would not seem suspicious if she told him about it later. Akiyama showed no reaction at all, as she had feared he might.

"Is that right? That must have been awful. Did you have enough money to get by?"

If Michiko had taken a moment to observe his expression carefully, she would have seen that, instead of anger, there was a look of joy in his eyes at the fact that she and Tsutomu had stayed the night together in a hotel.

Tomiko's lovemaking, which had been mixed with a touch of pity, encouraged this cowardly academic to indulge the illusion that theirs was a grand love. He had been gripped with a feeling of satisfaction all the way back from the lake at Kawaguchi. From time to time a faint smile played at the corners of his mouth. His taste for adultery, nurtured by his reading of French romances, had been sated.

It is truly one of the miracles of Western influence on contemporary Japan that this taste for adultery should obliterate a husband's jealousy over the possibility of his own wife's infidelity.

Michiko detected something in the casual attitude displayed by her forty-one-year-old husband—*Was it the way he sat in his chair? Was it the way he held his chopsticks?*—some indescribable sluggishness in his movements that was second nature to him now. His movements struck her as ugly somehow, but she did not have time to consider either the source of her feelings, or the cause of her husband's attitude. She had been surprised by his reaction, but she was relieved at the same time that she was not being blamed for having spent the night with Tsutomu.

She gave no further consideration to why she felt her husband was ugly. She did, however, reflect on her own joy at not being accused by him. That was Michiko's disposition. She would have Tsutomu move out of the house, even at the risk of driving him back to his former licentious lifestyle. In the end, Michiko was a sentimental egotist. She reasoned to herself that if Tsutomu went back to his old ways, he would commit his youthful indiscretions and that would be the end of it. Whereas if he were to make a mistake with her, he would destroy his life.

Three days after the storm she told Tsutomu he would have to leave. It was painful for her. She could not look him in the eye.

"I hope you understand how hard it is for me to say all this," she said, "but it's absolutely necessary if we don't want to ruin our relationship. For our own safety the only thing I can do is ask you to move somewhere else."

Tsutomu had been anticipating these words because Michiko had been avoiding him. He had been waiting constantly for a chance to embrace her, but no matter how much he hoped, he finally had to accept that she would never give her love to him.

He should never have hesitated that night. Had he crossed the line, everything would be different now. Michiko would not have been able to shut herself up inside her shell, as she always did. He thought he had been a fool, and he started to dislike Michiko, who could so coldly say the one thing that was most bitterly painful to him. The youthful Tsutomu was under the misapprehension that once he had made a woman his conquest, she would be his.

"You can talk all you want about how bitter this is for you," he said. "But you don't have it as hard as I do. I'm the one who has to leave. I know now that you don't love me, Mit-chan. No matter how hard it might be, it won't be as bad as having me stay on in this house."

"How can you say such a terrible thing? There's no other way for us."

"Did Akiyama say something?"

"He hasn't said a word. That's why I'm suffering."

"This is too much." Tsutomu stood up. His eyes were laughing, but his mouth was twisted. Seeing his face, Michiko felt her chest constrict. Nonetheless, she held to her convictions.

"Life is hard, yes," she said. "You ought to know that. You went to war."

"War is easy. All you have to do is look out for yourself. If that doesn't work out, you die. And that's the end of the story."

"So civilian life is harder than war? I can't accept that it's all right just to die. You have to understand that."

"I don't want to understand. But don't worry. I won't die after I'm kicked out of here. I'll respect your wishes. In the meantime, it'd be best if I learn to dislike you, Mit-chan."

Michiko started to cry.

"If you lose the income you get for tutoring Yukiko, you'll be in trouble. Let me at least pay you that much."

"Don't put yourself out." Tsutomu was genuinely angry. Her tears had not moved him at all. "Do you think I'd accept such help? It's insulting."

"I'm just thinking about you. Can't you at least understand that much?"

"I understand enough already."

Tsutomu quickly contacted a member of the old gang he used to play around with, and they agreed to share an apartment near Gotanda. As it turned out, this friend was always spending time at his girlfriend's house, so Tsutomu all but had the apartment to himself.

When he heard that Tsutomu was moving out, Akiyama looked a little disappointed. His reaction surprised Michiko.

Ōno was the most sentimental at the going-away party Michiko held at her house. He was a man who regretted the loss of anyone who was dependent on him. He assumed that Tsutomu was leaving because of Akiyama's discontent over having to support his wife's relative. As a husband, however, he had to acknowledge Akiyama's position. He encouraged Tsutomu to come and look after Yukiko's lessons as he had done before, but Tsutomu declined the offer.

Tomiko had more or less discerned the real reason behind all this. The only point she got wrong—and that on account of her jealousy—was her belief that something had actually happened between Tsutomu and Michiko at the hotel in Murayama.

Later she jokingly discussed this with Akiyama. Although he agreed with her opinion, he showed hardly any sign that he was jealous. Rather, he offended her when he laughed at her claim.

"You're the only one I love," he said, "so I couldn't care less what Michiko does."

"You're a liar." She tried to tell him off, but was shocked that Akiyama really was nonchalant about the whole affair. Akiyama intended to demonstrate his love for Tomiko in this way, but the real effect was to raise doubts about the durability of his emotions.

In Tomiko's mind, Tsutomu's move to his own apartment meant that she would be freer to try to get closer to him. Her intuition told her that something had happened between Michiko and Tsutomu. If they had to separate because they had an affair, then she believed that their relationship could not end in this way, that it was not over yet. Thus, she thought that in the interim, while they were apart, there might be an opening for her to squeeze between them.

Yukiko missed Tsutomu with all her heart. Tsutomu felt sad for this child, who was being warped into a spoiled brat by her indifferent father and willful mother. He believed there was nothing he could do for her, since his love for Michiko made it necessary for him to leave. Children are always sacrificed like this by adults. Resentments accumulate, unrecognized by anyone else, until eventually the child grows up with a highly developed aptitude for sacrificing others.

When Tsutomu left the following day, Michiko saw him off at the station. At the bend in the road where the tall trees of Hake disappear from view, Tsutomu stopped and looked back.

He remembered the time four months earlier when, having tired of all his affairs in Tokyo, he had come to Hake and gazed at those same trees from this same spot. He had innocently believed then that he would find refuge here, and had happily responded to Michiko's invitation to live at her house. The result was a painful love. Now he had to leave, taking his dissatisfaction with him. The stand of trees, which had been an image of comfort and happiness for him ever since he was a boy, was now a symbol of his discontent and envy. Who was to blame for this?

Tsutomu looked at Michiko. There were rings around her eyes, as though she had rapidly aged. She looked back at him. She was suffering too. Would her suffering be his sole comfort? Was it wrong to want to make this person happy? Did he lack the ability to make her happy? Had he been mistaken from the start to hope that making her happy would make him happy too?

As they walked on, white and purple rose of Sharon withered along both sides of the road, and blue-gray drake flies busily droned among the flowers.

As his train pulled out for Tokyo, Tsutomu knew he would never forget the figure of Michiko standing perfectly still outside the gate of the station, amid the striking long shadows of early autumn.

Tsutomu's apartment was halfway between Meguro and Gotanda. It stood on the cliffside of a bluff facing a ravine that the Megurogawa had carved on the western edge of the Musashino plateau. The bluff had been subdivided into lots during the time of the war in China in the 1930s, and was now covered with Western-style middle-class housing. Most of the houses had been requisitioned by the American occupation authorities. In the evenings jazz flooded out onto the darkened streets, and crowds of Japanese would wander quietly in the area. The neighborhood was tightly guarded.

A National Railway line cut through the tip of Meguro. It turned near this neighborhood into the basin of the Megurogawa and skirted the cliff. Its embankment, paying no heed to the ups and downs of the lowlands, ran level all the way to the elevated line at Gotanda station. The land on the cliffside was the last land in this area to be subdivided because the noise of the trains was loudest there. It was said that the owner of an ironworks in Shibaura, who was a little eccentric, came up with the idea of obtaining the subdivision's land on the cheap and putting up an apartment building for his mistress. The style of the building matched the middle-class housing in the neighborhood, and it was praised at first for being rather fashionable. But slowly the building became run-down, and after frequent changes in ownership there was now little to distinguish it from the cheap apartments that had escaped the fire bombings.

The apartment manager had initially been very choosy about renters, but during the war his strict standards became impractical and he could no longer be so selective. The building was eventually occupied by people whose lives in the metropolis required this kind of simple abode—that is, people with low monthly salaries, or hostesses, or mistresses. A man in his forties, an itinerant performer of ballads in the Naniwabushi style, occupied the apartment to the right of Tsutomu's. He lived in a six-mat room with his wife and his wife's younger sister. He had two children with each woman. On those rare occasions when he came home from touring, he seemed to take pleasure in constantly bickering with the sisters. The apartment to the left of Tsutomu's had the name of a single male occupant on its door, but there was never anyone home during the day. Every evening, a little past midnight, different women would come there with their men. The place rang with the laughter of young women; Tsutomu gathered that it was a communal apartment for a group of hostesses who worked the cheap cafes in the vicinity of Gotanda. This environment was, if anything, a comfort to the despairing Tsutomu.

In the view outside his window, which was partially obstructed by a thick growth of trees near the cliff, the heights of Togoshi-Ebara gently rose beyond the Megurogawa, which was channeled so that it flowed beyond the rail line. All around were burnt-out remains. When he saw the ruins of the fire bombings, the first thing the veteran Tsutomu became aware of was the ancient topography, which had been exposed by the destruction of human habitation. He saw nothing but the beauty of the cliff-edged ravine in the burnt-out ruins of the Yamanote section of Tokyo. Having despaired of humanity on the battlefield, he felt that everything should revert to nature.

Now, outside his window, he saw more and more barracks being erected in the ruins and light industry coming back to life. The Ikegami line was inaugurated from the upper floors of a department store connected to Gotanda station, and a block of buildings was constructed in the middle of the broad basin of the Megurogawa.

At night, when he was trying to sleep, he could hear the whine of trains slowly picking up speed as they left Meguro and Gotanda stations. The keening noise would increase by degrees from both directions, rending the air as the trains passed each other beneath his window, then diminishing in volume as they headed toward their respective destinations. In his present state of mind, this noise was agreeable to him.

He thought of Hake as some distant stage setting. Characters moved about like shadows among the quiet trees and houses of old Musashino. There was no life there. He had been deluded to have ever thought he could find peace in such a place.

Yet having breathed the air of Hake, something had changed inside Tsutomu. The student who had once announced her love for him came to his apartment one evening and stayed the night. The next morning she slapped his face and left, screaming, "I'm not some cheap whore!"

Tsutomu was furious and yelled "Bitch!" after her. This was the sole word of parting he gave in return for all the amusement she had provided him. There had been absolutely no emotion in his cruel lovemaking.

He rarely went to school. But in a switch for him he did take to reading books and keeping a few intellectual things around him.

Existentialism was fashionable at the time, but it seemed like a joke to him. Proponents of the philosophy spoke as though irrationality and ugliness were the privileges of humanity. A man like Tsutomu, who had had his fill of ugliness on the battlefield, could never bring himself to endorse such thinking. Petty existentialists prescribe their notion of existence as apheliotropic; but the idea of turning away from the sun brought them no honor, and was utterly unconnected to the things that drove existentialists to be diligent. He thought that no animal, including humans, lived in accord with such a notion of existence, but lived by ideals that their own biological needs embraced and nurtured.

Reportage and tales of adventurers who traveled abroad to Taiwan made him feel ill. Such writing expressed a lingering regret for things that had been rendered meaningless by Japan's demilitarization. The existence of opportunists who stacked their military scrip on the table of some restaurant at a base behind the lines in Burma, and who fired off their pistols for fun, was definitely ugly.

Communism had been the first ideology to attract his interest. But upon reading popular explanations of the movement's doctrines, which covered everything from the explanation of surplus value to historical materialism, he began to sniff out falsehoods. He had known the chaos of battle, and could not imagine any revolution proceeding in so orderly a fashion as some claimed. Histories of social movements were firmly supported by lies and expediencies that were in no way outdone by accounts of the war written during wartime. An impatient young man like Tsutomu was convinced that leaders at the end of the nineteenth century had brought about the wars of the first half of the twentieth by abandoning the courage of the barricade and opening Japan to the world.

After hearing Tsutomu's opinions, a budding student organizer who was in his class told him, "You sound like an anarchist. But those ideas were settled a long time ago. You may talk big, but you live on your father's inheritance, and your hands are spotless. A life may be nothing to regret once you're dead, but you'd kill yourself the moment you were arrested, afraid of having your fingernails ripped out under torture. At best, you were a minor officer in a brigade, and in the end you were taken advantage of by the reactionaries."

This young man, who looked like someone with a monthly stipend and who had spotless hands himself, turned his back on Tsutomu.

Tsutomu's aimless spirit inevitably turned to Hake and Michiko. There was a thick stand of trees on the cliffside near his apartment and, like Hake, there were many zelkova. The stiff, gnarly bark visible from his window was as hard as Michiko's heart. It left no traces even when it was scratched.

Having read some works on communism, he thought that Michiko's refusal was the result of the social condition of being a wife. Because he was still young, Tsutomu did not realize that social conditions do not always manifest themselves in the will of an individual.

He thought the self-control he exhibited at the hotel in Murayama was the result of habits imposed on the consciousness of ex-soldiers, whose initiative to act is taken from them. Everything he truly wanted to do was prohibited by society. His behavior that night at Murayama was a faint echo of a more general societal restraint. He was unaware that these ideas were merely a form of self-deception—for even as he longed to take action, he was in fact avoiding it.

By turning love into a societal concern, he was making his ideas lean in a direction that would kill love. And yet he could not block certain thoughts from his mind: *I wonder what Michiko is doing now? I wonder if she still thinks about me?* Love cannot be completely extinguished by ideologies.

The bluff was once the site of the villa of a feudal lord from the southwestern part of Honshu. The remains of the villa's garden, including its pond, were close to Tsutomu's apartment. This garden had been turned into a park, but few people had visited it during the war. The paths circling the pond and the Western-style pavilions were now overgrown and dilapidated. Tsutomu enjoyed this park because the pond and trees reminded him of Hake. He often took a nap on the lawn there.

The refreshing autumn air and the stagnant pond, filled with water plants, reminded him of the sound and glitter of the water flowing into the pond at Hake. He thought the solitary drake fly darting over the black water of the pond, lingering past its season, was an image of his own heart.

Tsutomu could not shake the feeling that he had made a mistake at Murayama. At the same time, he did not think he should have acted on his desire. His regrets piled up, and he gradually came to realize that he would always have regrets precisely because his mistake was irrevocable.

Whenever a book on Musashino caught his eye in a used bookstore, he bought it for his collection. He never tired of poring over the photographs in these books of the trees, flowers, and grasses of Musashino. He realized that these images, which had been touched up by the photographers, did not necessarily match actual perceptions. He could not help taking pleasure in these images, but his pleasure only deepened his longing.

One morning in October, the clouds cleared in the sky beyond the heights at Ebara, which he could survey from his window, and Mt. Fuji became visible. Sitting snugly, like some little confectionery, just above the disordered, burnt-out horizon, it appeared smaller than when he viewed it from Hake. Tsutomu remembered that once, at Hayama, he had seen an image of unchanging love in the elegant cone of the volcano. Every day, from that morning on, as soon as he got up he would search for Mt. Fuji along the horizon.

Chapter 10

A Husband's Rights

Beneath the weathered roof at Hake, Michiko was thinking about Tsutomu. Her practical concerns were limited exclusively to her misgivings—that he would quickly run through the inheritance from his father because he had lost his income as a tutor; that the constraints on his lifestyle would force him to rely on a meal-ticket diner for his food. Moreover, she was forever trembling with the fear that his former, dissolute lifestyle would become even more intense now that he was living unencumbered in that apartment.

Her own self-control had been justified. If there had been circumstances under which she could be together with Tsutomu, then she would have given him her own paltry possessions. But such immoral behavior could never end well, even in a society that no longer punished adultery. On top of all that, she was five years older than Tsutomu. In another five years signs of age would show on her that a man in his twenties would find hard to accept. She couldn't bear to think that Tsutomu might someday have to put up with such a situation.

Living with Akiyama day after day became increasingly intolerable after Tsutomu left. At the beginning of their life together Michiko had always defended Akiyama. Her attitude stemmed partly from her willfulness toward her parents and second brother, who had opposed the marriage. But the role she had been playing as the daughter who leaves home was meaningless now that everyone in her family was dead. Her existence since their deaths was for the most part a prolongation of old habits, and perhaps her feelings of affection for her cousin had been transformed into love because of the void that had opened in her life. Once she began to have such feelings, she could no longer maintain her old habits.

She concluded that she had been only playacting the role of wife with a man she did not love. The restraint she had exercised with Tsutomu was just an extension of that role.

Had she revealed her true self by nearly giving in to Tsutomu at Murayama? She justified asking Tsutomu to leave her house by claiming she was thinking of his future. But wasn't her request in fact motivated by the fear that she would lose his love some day?

She came to believe that everyone around her was playing their respective roles. Akiyama and Ōno were playacting their roles as husbands. Tomiko, despite being a chronic flirt, played the role of wife at those times when her marriage to Ōno meant something to her.

Her late father had played his role as head of the house. His pedantic stoicism and cynicism had been mere affectations meant to conceal his boredom with playacting. Now, for the first time, Michiko understood why her oldest brother had rebelled against their father and led the life of a wanderer.

Neither her oldest brother nor her second brother, the pianist who died so young, had reached the age when they would have had to assume a role. Tsutomu too, she thought, was at that stage in his life, and she finally recognized the nature of her love for him. She seemed to have been born to be absorbed in such people. If Tsutomu maintained that sort of character his whole life, couldn't they find happiness together? Wouldn't the moral judgment of society be of no consequence to them? Thinking about things in this manner, her own ideas had become incongruous to her.

The notion of playacting taught her to observe her surroundings from a different perspective. She developed an interest in measuring just how perfectly people played their roles. Akiyama, apparently, was not completely faithful to the role of husband. When he went off to work, or went into his study, he was the perfect husband. On the other hand, considering his dislike of Tsutomu, which was truly beyond the pale, he wasn't really a self-sufficient head of the household. His recent behavior with Tomiko didn't seem normal either.

She forgave her husband because she could not satisfy him. Her self-deprecation prevented her from completely fulfilling her role as wife. In the end, she was convinced that nothing serious could ever happen between her husband and Tomiko because they were each constrained by the respective roles they had to play.

Her conclusions were only partly accurate. Only people who have the inclination to play a role are conscious of the fact that they are playing one. The objects of Michiko's concern just happened to be the kind of people most lacking that inclination.

For Tomiko, playing the role of a wife bound to a husband for financial reasons was a pretense she maintained for herself and for others.

Following their trip to the lake at Kawaguchi, Tomiko went twice with Akiyama to an inn in Shinjuku. After that she refused to go with him, no matter how much he pleaded. Akiyama had enough wit about him to see that underlying Tomiko's conventional excuse—"I have a husband and child"—was a lack of love for him. This did not diminish his feelings for her in the least. Desires that have been long suppressed can lead people to extravagant fantasies.

Having said nothing about the details of the inheritance of the Miyaji estate until this point in the story, it may seem a little offhand to bring it up now. Nonetheless, an incident happened that makes it necessary to mention the matter here.

The disposition of the estate was complicated. The second son, Keiji, died after Michiko had married Akiyama, and the common practice in such a case would have been to name the children of Michiko and Akiyama as heirs. But because they had no children, there was no legal heir, and the matter became a problem. Akiyama had hinted from time to time that perhaps he ought to be granted status as heir, but Michiko's father wouldn't agree to convene a family meeting. His excuse was always, "You'll probably have a child in the meantime." When he died in late 1946, the survivors agreed that Michiko would be designated the heir.

The estate, which consisted mainly of the land and buildings, was assessed inheritance taxes equal to nearly half the value of the property. Michiko proposed selling off the land at the top of the hillside to pay the taxes, but Akiyama argued that she should not be too quick to let such an out-of-the-way piece of land go because she would take a loss. He suggested that he advance her the money for the estate taxes from the royalties of his translations. He consulted Ōno, who was impressed by the plan. However, Akiyama later told Michiko that, in exchange for the money, he wanted the responsibility of trustee.

Because Michiko had always thought that the estate would belong to her husband, she replied that it made no difference to her. But when she casually mentioned Akiyama's suggestion to Ōno, he was adamantly opposed. Her father had not trusted his son-in-law, and so had made use of the special laws for designating an heir in order to leave everything to Michiko. Akiyama had told Ōno directly that he would advance the money to Michiko, but at the same time he was privately suggesting to Michiko that he be appointed trustee for the estate. Ōno thought this was a crafty way to operate, and told Michiko that under the civil code, which would be revised in the near future, the estate would automatically go to her. He also said that she had no reason to feel hesitant about the matter, and that it was better for him to advance her the money. She had to protect the estate on her own, and though he couldn't help much, he would advise her. This suggestion put Michiko on her guard about Ōno.

It was strange that both men wanted to administer such a small estate. She was holding on to it only because it was just the house and land; if necessary, she would sell it. She did not think Akiyama had the knack for managing the estate. He was, after all, a college professor. But she was also old-fashioned and would have felt sorry for her husband if he did not receive some portion of the inheritance. They depended on her husband's cash income for their monthly living expenses; and if he paid off the tax for her, then it was perfectly reasonable to transfer into his name some portion of the estate equal, at market value, to the amount he paid. When she mentioned this to Ōno, he laughed at her.

"You're a trusting soul," he said. "But you're all alone. No parents, no brothers. Can't you see that you have to keep the estate if you want Akiyama to treat you with respect?"

Michiko hated bringing such considerations into her marriage. Ōno, after all, was an outsider, and she was determined that certain matters should remain between husband and wife. At her own discretion she offered to transfer a portion of the estate to Akiyama equal to what he would pay for the taxes. She was surprised, therefore, when he turned her down, saying the arrangement was too cold and formal. Akiyama proposed instead that he be given the power of attorney to transfer the estate to his name. This would allow him to protect his investment by giving him the ability to dispose of the property in case something happened to Michiko. She was further surprised when he added that he wanted his power of attorney to apply to the house.

The house made up roughly half the estate, and its value was exactly equal to the percentage of the inheritance tax that Akiyama had advanced Michiko. She knew that the estate was assessed far below market price, and that she would have to keep an eye on her husband, just as Ōno had warned her. But when all was said and done, the whole thing turned out to be a tremendous bother, and so she agreed to Akiyama's proposal. And that is why her husband abandoned her.

A husband who supports his wife has two rights. He has the right to rape her and the right to leave her. These rights are never exercised so long as love remains between husband and wife. But when love is gone, the wife either has to submit or be divorced.

By obtaining the power of attorney to transfer the house to his name, the foundation of his marriage to Michiko was undermined by half. And so Akiyama, who had lost his head over Tomiko, began to drop frequent hints during his lovers' quarrels with her that he was going to divorce his wife. His words meant nothing to Tomiko, so long as she had no passion for him and Ōno earned enough to support her whims. But Ōno's business dealings had become increasingly risky of late, and when Michiko lost what was left of her estate, the situation became urgent.

Ōno's soap factory had been struggling for some time, ever since the supply of raw materials tightened and the company's market share declined. The scarcity of resources gradually eased with the end of the war, but the start-up of production had been sluggish. As things picked up, larger firms were given priority for allotments of imported whale oil and coconut oil. Restrictions were placed on the activities of black-market brokers, making it harder for small factories like Ōno's, which relied on the black market to compete. Ōno's special business skill—his innate boyish daring—had been a good, if accidental, fit with the loose practices of the wartime economy. Now that skill was betraying him.

His company was formed originally when the factory became independent during the dispersal of assets at the end of the war. Having managed the factory during the war, he became the new company head, though he held stock in name only. His profiteering lifestyle had been sustained mainly by misappropriating company funds. As long as sales were good, he was able to get by. But when sales went bad all the money he had squandered on extravagances began to affect his present lifestyle. He was buried in debt, unable to pay even the interest on the money he had borrowed on the black market.

He started by borrowing small amounts from acquaintances—a thousand yen here, two thousand yen there—until he had borrowed the maximum limit. He put his house up as collateral for a loan, and when all that money was gone he set his sights on Michiko's land. He proposed to pay her ten percent interest per month if she allowed him to use the land as security. His plan—especially his request that she keep all of it secret from her husband—frightened Michiko. The plan struck her as odd, but she was not the kind of woman who could refuse a request from her cousin. She decided she could give the interest payment to Tsutomu to compensate him for the loss of his monthly stipend for tutoring Yukiko.

Michiko was unaware that a portion of the first month's interest payment she received from Ōno had been paid from money he had secretly borrowed from Akiyama. Akiyama took perverse delight in lending money to a man he was cuckolding, but he did not know that his own wife was setting that same money aside. When Ōno took Yukiko on their trip to the Kyoto-Osaka region, he took all the money he had borrowed with Michiko's land as security. He gave the entire amount to a petroleum broker, who promptly absconded with it three days later.

From the day he married Michiko, Akiyama had felt oppressed by the Miyaji family. He had made his own way in the world, rising from a poor peasant family by educating himself. He was convinced that the magnanimity of the elder Miyaji and of his brothers-in-law was simply a product of their wealth, and he was made to feel inferior to them even on the most mundane occasions. When he married Michiko, he chose to live in a house as far away from Miyaji as he could get. His lingering sense of inferiority made it very difficult to get him to agree to move to the house at Hake, in spite of the danger of fire bombings closing in on Japan. He felt the same sense of inferiority toward Michiko, even when he was living alone with her.

Despite his sentiments—and even after he had tired of Michiko's body—Akiyama tried to maintain a life with her because the Miyaji family, which had lost its male children, had taken the unusual step of naming Michiko heir. He managed to get control of half the estate. When he found out that she had lost the remaining portion, she naturally became a totally useless dependent to him. At that moment the inferiority he had felt in the presence of the Miyaji family, including Michiko, was transformed into a feeling of sweet revenge. Now he could exercise a husband's right of divorce.

Akiyama learned from Tomiko that Michiko had secretly allowed Ōno to use her land as security for a loan, and that Ōno then promptly lost the money. She would never have told Akiyama if Ōno, distracted by the slump in his business, hadn't made use of one of his rights as a husband—that is, the right to have his way physically with a recalcitrant wife.

Ōno's business rapidly fell apart after he foolishly lost Michiko's money on his trip. He had been extravagantly entertaining people just two months earlier, and now he was reduced to selling his belongings to make ends meet. Furniture and antiques rapidly disappeared from the house because he had to keep up appearances, such as sending Yukiko to an expensive school. He had already hit up Tomiko's relatives for loans in private, and he finally reached the point where he had to ask her to sell her kimonos. Their marriage, which they had maintained to bolster Ōno's position, was now in danger.

Ōno, who had always taken pleasure in his wife's flirtations with other men, became violently jealous. He brought up all the old grudges he held against Akiyama, and even against Tsutomu, who was no longer at Hake. At some point he slipped from drinking sake to drinking hard, cheap *shōchū*. He got very drunk every night and insisted that Tomiko prove her love.

Tomiko had never loved Ōno, but she had continued living with him because he allowed her a degree of freedom, and because he had been largely undemanding about their sex life. Without these conditions, her life with him became intolerable.

Tomiko would resist having sex with Ōno. Usually their struggle ended in defeat for him, but it would carry over to the next day. This hellish situation was repeated night after night. Whenever Ōno won, his success essentially took the form of a violent rape.

All this worked to Akiyama's advantage. He no longer had to mention his plan to divorce Michiko to start up his trysts with Tomiko again. One day Tomiko surprised him by calling on him at his college. Their meeting, however, did not bring the affection he expected. Tomiko simply wanted a rest.

The chaos in Ōno's house attracted Michiko's attention as well. She had to listen to Ōno's constant complaints, while Akiyama listened to Tomiko at the inn in Shinjuku.

"It's so bad I'd divorce Ōno now if it weren't for Yukiko," she told him.

In Akiyama's eyes, Tomiko's complaints reduced her value as a lover, but her resolve to divorce Ōno gave him a new opportunity to become her companion. It was during one of their rendezvous, when the talkative Tomiko was telling him about Ōno's finances, that she revealed how Ōno had used Michiko's land as security and then let the money slip away. The revelation made him hopeful rather than angry.

By the time he got home and confronted Michiko, however, he vented his anger out of force of habit as a husband. Now that Tomiko wasn't there in front of him, he regretted the loss of the property after all.

"Why did you do that without speaking to me?" he demanded.

"I'm sorry, but I thought if I told you, you wouldn't let me do it."

"Of course I wouldn't. I know that Ōno's up to no good."

"But I felt sorry for him. If he's got a problem, it's my problem too."

"Charity has limits. Lending him so much...we're the ones who'll have to pay the interest to keep the property from slipping away."

Akiyama finally came to this realization as he was getting worked up. Then he became truly enraged. Michiko finally understood the enormity of the situation.

"Ōno paid me some interest," she said, "so let's use that."

"You've been hiding that, too? When did he pay you?"

"He gave me three thousand yen last month. I was supposed to get more, but..."

Akiyama was dumbfounded. "That was money he borrowed from me!"

Michiko had to endure words of abuse she had never heard from her husband. She began to cry, and appealed to him.

"One way or the other, I had no choice at the time but to let him use the land," she said. "He's my cousin, after all. If that's wrong, then I don't care what happens."

"You're a naïve fool."

"Who told you about this?"

Akiyama was flustered. "Never mind who told me. What you've done is a lot worse than snitching."

He ran off to confer with Ōno. All he got was a clichéd apology and some empty promises.

Thereafter began a period of pride and vengeance for Akiyama, and a period of torment for Michiko. Even as Akiyama was forfeiting the right to call himself a husband by continuing his trysts with Tomiko, he pointed out repeatedly that Michiko was not a perfect wife. Akiyama criticized her, dredging up her relationship with Tsutomu. He knew she was still thinking about Tsutomu. He had been aware for some time that whenever the two of them had sex, which he demanded of her occasionally, Michiko never opened her eyes. So he forced her to keep them open. And to keep his perverse pleasure fresh, he would intentionally demand sex on those days when meeting Tomiko was impossible.

Tsutomu stopped visiting Hake altogether, so Michiko had to put up with everything on her own. She did not particularly want to meet Tsutomu, or have him listen to her. She didn't even write him a letter. Entangled for the first time in her life in financial difficulties, everything connected with Tsutomu seemed like a distant dream to her.

Akiyama, as always, was considering a divorce, but then Tomiko expressed her opposition to the idea.

"People can't get divorced just like that, " she said. "I'm not really sure I can get divorced, now that Ōno is ruined."

"Then what about us?"

"What about us? Nothing, that's what. We'll just have to go on like this," she sneered. Akiyama had recently begun to give her an allowance. Even if she managed to get a divorce from Ōno and gain her freedom, she didn't want to go to Akiyama's place. She wanted to go to Tsutomu's.

One day she visited Tsutomu's apartment. She brought with her a floor cushion she had sewn from scraps of cloth.

"Your place is a mess. How can you stand it?" She opened a window. "Here. This is for you." She laid the cushion on the floor and sat down.

Tsutomu looked at Tomiko with gentle eyes, because she brought with her the atmosphere of Hake.

He was shocked to hear about the situation there. Tomiko played down the story of Michiko's pathetic circumstances so as not to arouse his sympathy. Even so, he felt sad. *Why doesn't Michiko call me?* he thought. *I may not be able to help, but I could at least listen to her. Have I become so unimportant?*

Tomiko of course exaggerated her own problems. She even told him details of her intimate life with Ōno that were inappropriate to mention to a bachelor like Tsutomu.

Same old Tomiko, Tsutomu thought. *You ought to know by now you can't fool me with your tricks.*

Sitting face-to-face with her in his isolated apartment, he couldn't help being attracted to her in a way that was different from his feelings for her at Hake when they talked together in the company of Ōno and Yukiko. After she had begun her affair with Akiyama, a kind of luster, arising from despair, had appeared in her face, which was worn and gaunt as a result of her financial hardships.

He recalled the moonlit night in the garden when their hands were entwined. Tomiko did not bring it up, but he felt that her suggestive laughter, mingled with her casual talk, alluded to that moment.

In any case, she was married to someone else. Suffering from an unrequited love for a severe and proper wife, Tsutomu found the flirting of this faithless wife charming enough that, at a time when the difficult thing he really wanted was unavailable to him, he could be captivated by a superficial resemblance.

Tsutomu, who read books, was inclined to think that Michiko's rejection of him was based solely upon her status as a wife. If the desire to overcome her rejection were the source of his obsession, then perhaps having an affair with Tomiko would, at the very least, free him from that obsession.

In spite of himself, Tsutomu felt as though he was waiting for something from Tomiko. She noticed his mood, but her womanly instinct was to retreat if a man made a move toward her. Giving herself over to the good feelings stimulated at the moment by her flirting, she forgot all about the hopes she had been clinging to when she arrived earlier.

"You've changed a little, Tsutomu."

"How have I changed?"

"It's nothing important, but you look pale."

She stood up.

Tsutomu walked with her as far as the station. In keeping with his taciturn nature, his footsteps were quiet, and he seemed hesitant. For Tomiko his footsteps were more than adequate recompense for the humiliation she had suffered from Tsutomu's rejections.

They stopped and stood on the hillside overlooking the heights of Ebara and the block of buildings at Gotanda station rising before them.

"I like gazing out at things," she said.

"What do you gaze at?"

"Everything. I like looking at everything from up high. It gives me the feeling I can do anything."

"I feel the same way."

Tsutomu thought that he must definitely make up for this humiliation.

CHAPTER 11

A CAMERA'S TRUTH

Akiyama continued to meet Tomiko in secret. Although he began to feel that their trysts didn't quite amount to the love he had always dreamed of, the mysterious effect of their intimacy over time was to make Tomiko hard for him to forget—an effect which signifies something other than love. Rendered vulnerable by his emotional inclinations, this professor was enraptured, for example, by the expression Tomiko made when she refused his demands—the ferocity in her eyes as she tenaciously kept her face down, all the while darting glances up at him. Once he started slipping down the slope of his passions he couldn't stop, and it didn't matter whether it was love or not. It was all the same to him.

Tomiko was half-desperate. The money Akiyama gave her—a thousand, two thousand yen from time to time—was hardly enough to meet her household expenses, but it helped, like a lubricant, to smooth things over in a pinch. That became her excuse to keep seeing him. In fact, she had grown accustomed to their tête-à-têtes, and actually began to look forward to them. Their trysts were the only times when she could escape from her troubles and her wretchedness.

She felt no guilt over Michiko. Tomiko had once had a lover, so marriage was a formality that certainly posed no hindrance to doing whatever she wanted. Partly out of curiosity, she went over to Michiko's place just to observe her face. Her curiosity mingled with the pleasure of secret revenge she felt concerning Tsutomu. She exaggerated the details of her visit to his new apartment, and rejoiced to see how Michiko's face hardened.

Michiko could not help seeing that whenever Akiyama and Tomiko were together, an intimacy seemed to spring up spontaneously between them. For example, if Michiko excused herself and left the room to do some errand, the moment she came back the two of them would stop talking and stare at her. Michiko was startled to see the same sarcastic expression in their flashing eyes.

She remembered that she had once seen them standing together, looking out on the garden with their backs to her. For some reason it looked to her as if they were snuggling. She put the matter down to her own inferiority complex, but the scene mysteriously kept coming back to her.

She had always reproached herself for her emotional indifference toward Akiyama, and had believed it was wrong to be worried about his receptiveness to Tomiko's flirtatiousness. In fact, she had not really minded his reactions all that much until she almost lost herself to Tsutomu. After that, she no longer trusted herself; and when she lost her faith in herself, she could no longer trust anyone else. One more emotion came into play concerning her feelings toward her husband. She felt compelled to blame him for not being worthy of her. Having controlled herself with Tsutomu, she could not forgive her husband's lack of self-control.

If Akiyama and Tomiko were having an affair, Michiko wouldn't be able to forgive Tomiko either. Quite apart from her own shame, she had to consider that Ōno was a cousin she had known since childhood. He deserved to be criticized for how he had behaved recently, but he would be in worse trouble if Tomiko could not be strong for him. Michiko had been offended once when Tomiko had boasted about the dowry and pin money she'd brought with her when she was married. For her to behave self-ishly like that again, now that Ōno was in difficulty, would be too terrible, especially with Yukiko to consider.

Michiko was miserable at having to tell herself over and over that these worries did not mean she was jealous. Having to confront the truth that she was in love with Tsutomu made her suffering even greater.

Because Michiko had been preoccupied with worries about the estate, she had briefly forgotten about Tsutomu. Now that she was worried about her husband's affair, her heart turned again to love.

Tsutomu was still in love with Michiko, but his despair had awakened a perverse willfulness in him. Sensing that he had been mocked by Tomiko, he was at a loss for several days after her visit. He gradually convinced himself that he should take advantage of Tomiko's offer in order to free himself from his hopeless love for Michiko.

The time to act is when you are in doubt. This was a lesson drilled into him at the front. He had no way of knowing when Tomiko would come again, so he decided to set out for Hake. It had been almost a month since his last visit, so Michiko would not be angry with him. *What do I care if she gets mad?* he thought. *She doesn't love me anyway.*

He put on the same airman's clothes he'd worn when he went to Hake in June. There was, however, one difference in his attire. A camera was slung across his shoulders. It was one of those cheap Japanese models that the friend with whom Tsutomu shared the apartment had left behind when he moved to his girlfriend's place. Tsutomu was constantly thinking about Michiko and Hake. He would go out and take photographs of the vestiges of old Musashino in the vicinity of his apart-ment—zelkova, black alder, and sumac trees, and the sparse pampas grass thrusting up amid the stones of burnt-out ruins. When he decided to visit Hake again, he brought the camera along to take pictures of the things there that were fixed in his memory. His desire to take such photographs had little connection with his aim of drawing closer to Tomiko, but indicated that he continued to feel an attachment to Michiko. And sure enough, his heart was overcome by a powerful surge of happiness as he left the station and approached Hake. He completely forgot why he had come here in the first place.

His feet, of their own accord, carried him past Tomiko's house and on toward Michiko's. The thick shapes of the stand of trees at Hake looked as if they were submerged beneath the bright October sky. He turned the camera toward that distant prospect.

The rear wooden door he had entered once was as old and decayed as ever. The damp skirt of the hill was coated in a blue-green moss like scattered powder. He took a picture of that as well.

The wooden door, however, was locked tight. On the very day Michiko decided to ask Tsutomu to leave, she had placed a padlock on the door. When he realized it had been locked from the inside, anger instinctively surged in him, and he shook the door two or three times.

The hollow at Hake was not just a crossing for birds and butterflies. It was a path for people as well. The ancient road, which peasants had constructed by scraping the reddish soil off to one side, bordered the lot of the Miyaji house as it descended into the Nogawa basin. He started down the road, his long strides giving the impression that he was running. Along the way the cries of a flock of magpies echoed through the tops of the cedars. There was a row of well-tended osmanthus trees at the bottom of the slope in front of the Miyaji house, which faced south. The trees were in full bloom, showing their final flowers of the season. Walking amidst their choking fragrance, Tsutomu's anger was suffused with a sweet melancholy.

His voice, calling from the veranda, echoed through the seemingly vacant house. Someone stirred within, then Michiko's figure appeared in the dark threshold. Tsutomu went straight up to her.

Michiko's lips did not resist, but slowly the strength came back to her hands, which she had placed on Tsutomu's chest as if to support herself. When they finally pulled far enough apart to be able to make out each other's features, Tsutomu saw all the misfortune on her thin, wide-eyed face.

"Why didn't you call me?" His breath caught in his throat.

Michiko did not answer. Tears were flowing. Tsutomu could only put his arms around her shoulders and help her sit down. Her heart was beating, echoing like noises reverberating in the old house.

"Akiyama is behaving terribly," he said. "I've heard he's bullying you about money."

"It's my own fault. I lost everything. I really thought I might be able to help you out." She could finally force a smile.

"That's ridiculous. I don't need anything. But to tell the truth, I'm glad you're broke. Now Akiyama can't say my feelings are motivated by greed."

"That doesn't matter. You always think such strange things."

Michiko slowly calmed down as her big-sisterly feelings returned.

"This won't do. What if someone drops by?" At last she was able to push away the hands that were trying to hold her.

Was this wrong? Tsutomu felt despair piercing his emptiness. *Was it wrong to think the estate means nothing, that only our love is important? It can't be that she doesn't love me. Her eyes and lips tell me she does. Maybe her problems make it impossible for her even to consider that this is the only way to happiness.*

Because he was so young, Tsutomu did not realize that to remind Michiko of her misfortune so soon after they embraced, groping like two blind people, would only make her retreat inside her shell.

He was sure that Akiyama and Tomiko had continued betraying Michiko after their trip at the end of the summer, but he didn't say anything to Michiko. He believed that talking about her husband's affair would wound her to no purpose, since she was trying to control her feelings for him. At the same time, Akiyama was making her miserable, and so Tsutomu thought it would be best to speak his mind if that would get her away from here.

"Has it occurred to you that Akiyama may have some other reason for going on about money the way he does?"

"Some other reason?"

"I'm talking about Tomiko." He blurted it out, but grew fearful when he saw Michiko's face grow cold and hard. Her expression, however, quickly relaxed.

"I'm more likely to know about that than you. You want to tell me that we can do what we want because Akiyama is selfish. But what he does has no bearing on how we behave."

Whenever Michiko thought about her situation, she was quite capable of feeling the unhappiness of a woman playing the role of a virtuous wife. But when she met Tsutomu, she always felt compelled to adhere to that role. This was the distinctive characteristic of her unhappy love. In order to drive thoughts of Akiyama and Tomiko from her mind, she had to think about Tsutomu. But when Tsutomu was there with her, she had to trample on her feelings for him.

"Then I guess I'll have to accept what I've known all along," said Tsutomu. "That you don't love me."

"That's not true. I have to behave properly for your sake."

"But you're not really thinking of me. You're just hurting me."

"You should be able to endure anything. After all, you're the one who brags so much about all your hardships during the war."

"There's nothing more important than being happy and not suffering. The best way to achieve happiness is to grow strong together. Who cares about conventional morality?"

"Our only strength is in morality. You have to understand that much for me."

"Even if I say I understand, nothing will come of it," he said. "There will never be a time when we can be happy. Whatever there is between us will never be moral enough to satisfy you."

But Michiko was in love. Her face blushing from shame, she took his hand and said, "I do love you. Please believe me. I just want to do things I can live with."

"You only love yourself."

Michiko wavered. Tsutomu's words raised the very doubt that had been flitting through her mind. Even so, she felt she had to hold onto her ideal of love. For Michiko, loving oneself and loving another were one and the same. If you cannot be loved for who you are, just as you are, then love has no value.

"You're wrong," she said. "I just want you to become like me."

"If I think like you do, we'll spend our whole lives apart just to uphold moral values."

"There are things more important than morality."

"Such as?" He put the question to her harshly.

"A vow."

"A vow?"

"If we promise to truly love one another, to never waver and to always keep our vow, a time will come when the rules of society change and we can live together without shame."

Tsutomu gazed at her, entranced by the vital spirit in her haggard face as she spoke. It struck him as both a sign of new hope and the final radiance of despair.

"How long will we have to wait?"

"I don't know. Five years. Ten years. Even if it takes our whole lives, it's for the best."

"It is for the best, isn't it." Tsutomu had lost all hope.

"Will you promise me?"

"I promise."

What was the point of their vow? Tsutomu wondered. *Michiko was wrong. A vow ought to be made only before the gods.*

Tsutomu simply thought that Michiko's relationship with Akiyama would change over time, and that he would eventually be able to protect Michiko himself.

"Please hold me," she said.

They kissed a long time, gazing into each other's eyes to test the firmness of their vow. Tsutomu told himself that if Michiko was satisfied with this, he would have to be satisfied as well.

But is it really right to be satisfied? Is it right to follow always the wishes of Michiko's heart? Would it be wrong to ask her if there isn't something more important in our kisses than this vow? Doubts arose in Tsutomu's heart just as Michiko pushed him away.

"Please go now," she said. "Let's leave it at this. Akiyama will be back soon. I don't want to see you two together today."

"May I come when he's not around?"

"No, that's out of the question. It wouldn't be right if you can't visit in a way that's open and legitimate. I'll send letters to tell you when you can come. Is that all right? Please come when I write."

"So you'll be sure to invite me at least once a month?" Tsutomu spoke with a hint of sarcasm.

"Yes. About once a month. Come to think of it, why did you drop by today?" Michiko's sudden return to more mundane concerns flustered Tsutomu. His visit had not gone at all the way he had anticipated.

"No reason really," he said. "It'd been a while, and I was concerned, and I wanted to take some photos."

"Photos? What for?"

"Because I miss the scenery around here."

Tsutomu found comfort in Michiko's gentle eyes.

"Let me take a picture of you. I miss you a lot more than the scenery."

"Stop it. You shouldn't say such things."

Despite her protests, she went down into the garden as Tsutomu directed and stood under the eaves, where some untended chrysanthemums were flowering.

Looking at her through the viewfinder, Tsutomu could hardly believe his eyes. Michiko's face was even more noticeably haggard in the sunlight. The many wrinkles creasing the corners of her eyes and her cheeks stood out clearly. Because of his youthful sensibility, he shuddered in spite of himself.

"You're dropping by Ōno's place, aren't you?" Michiko said. "Eiji's finances have improved a little recently. The managing director of another company, Mr. Yagi, has apparently put all the loans in order and taken over the factory. Eiji will step down and become a regular director. He says he'll live on his retainer's fee for a while. It looks like the only money that will be lost for good is the money I lent him."

"This must be rough on Tomiko."

"She told me she went to your place."

"She brought me a floor cushion."

Tomiko had not mentioned the cushion to anyone. It came as a slight shock to Michiko.

"Be careful on your way," she said.

"You're not going over with me?"

"I wouldn't feel right."

Michiko looked prim and stiff. The "wife" apparent in her manner showed just how deeply rooted she was in her everyday life with Akiyama, in spite of her vow. Tsutomu was hurt.

Michiko stood at the edge of the veranda, watching Tsutomu's figure retreat as he headed back through the osmanthus. She gazed after his vigorous, dance-like steps with a sense of foreboding. She was no longer able to look at him again with the eyes of a big sister.

Her sense of foreboding was well-founded. He immediately forgot about their vow. This was due in part to the choking smell of the osmanthus, and in part to the effect of viewing Michiko's face in the sunlight. He thought, *What possible meaning could her promise have for me? To hold onto our feelings and wait until there's a change in social values—isn't that the same as giving in to society? I don't think the world will change so quickly or that morals will be revised any time soon. In the meantime we'll grow old, and people will laugh at us if we talk about love. Isn't she already old?*

The sweet osmanthus was flowering in the part of the garden that bordered the lower road at Hake, flooding it with a pungent smell. Tsutomu caught this scent again from the sweet osmanthus Ōno had received from Michiko's father and planted on both sides of the gate to his house.

The osmanthus at Michiko's was a type also known as devilwood, but the trees at Tomiko's were a different kind known as Asian osmanthus. On a whim Ōno had asked his uncle to transplant only a single variety.

The white flowers of the trees showed clearly against the green lawn. Tsutomu always felt that he was entering a different world whenever he came here from the old Miyaji house.

He remembered his original purpose for coming. The vow he had made with Michiko should have rendered that purpose meaningless. But on the way over, as he walked through the Asian osmanthus and neared the eaves of Tomiko's house, his doubts about the vow prompted him to find an excuse to give in to Tomiko's seduction.

If our vow is a fantasy, then I'll have to take Tomiko away from Akiyama. That way he'll always stay with Michiko. That will be my one kind act toward Michiko. This was the train of Tsutomu's thought. Desire frequently masquerades as morality.

Tomiko was alone. The maid had been dismissed some time ago, and in the lonely rooms there were traces on the walls and *tatami* mats where furnishings had once been. Tomiko nevertheless got up cheerfully and went out to meet Tsutomu.

"What a surprise! What wind blew you in here?" She spoke in the same old flippant tone, shrugging her shoulders.

"Nice view."

Tsutomu sat down on the edge of the veranda and gazed out at the Nogawa basin, where rice fields were turning yellow, at the long ridge of mountains in Tama, and at the Tanzawa massif, which revealed all its folds in the transparent autumn air. Mt. Fuji appeared close behind those mountains, as if it was clinging to them. "Pure and graceful." The shape of Fuji, framed in a sky like clear glass, looked exactly the way it was described in this classical epithet used by so many ancient poets.

His praise for the scenery they were viewing was a roundabout jab intended to excite her. When Tomiko visited his apartment and they were looking at the block of buildings at Gotanda station, she had said, "I like gazing out at things." The clear view of the fields and mountains, however, made him forget his secret desires. And by now Tomiko had forgotten all about what she had said then.

"Were you at Michiko's house?" she said.

"Yes. She's looks very thin."

"Ōno's been a real pain. I've grown thinner too, haven't I? Look what the kitchen work's done to my hands. It's all Ōno's fault that we're in such a sorry state."

"I heard things had gotten better lately."

"Michiko told you that. But it turns out there were all kinds of secret loans. We're living hand to mouth now, selling things just to eat. I thought maybe we could win the lottery, so I sold a kimono the other day and bought ten tickets. Not one of them hit the jackpot."

"You'd have a better chance finding money on the ground than winning the lottery. So Akiyama is the richest one now?"

Tsutomu did not miss the shadow that flashed across Tomiko's face.

"I doubt it," she said. "Michiko doesn't look so well-off."

"I'm sure they need money for something else."

Tomiko stood up without replying and went to prepare some tea. Watching the movements of her slender hips beneath the plain everyday silk of her clothing, Tsutomu realized he had been deluding himself. He thought he was drawn to Tomiko because she was an uncomplicated wife compared to Michiko; but Tomiko's attraction was merely the aimless power emitted by the body of a woman who is possessed by a man and whose desires have reached the point of saturation.

Tomiko placed the tea in front of Tsutomu, sat down properly, and smiled.

"Tsutomu? Are you here to spy for someone?"

Caught off guard by this thrust, Tsutomu was unable to parry.

"It's not like you to try to sound someone out."

"Why would I do that? Can't I show a little concern for you and Akiyama?"

"You're lying," said Tomiko. "You're not concerned about me at all."

The moment she'd seen Tsutomu walking through the osmanthus in the distance, Tomiko had detected a sharp light in his eyes she had never seen before. She knew that light very well. It was in the eyes of most of the men who looked at her. Although it was in his eyes now, she found it rather uninteresting.

Tsutomu acted with the confidence he had acquired from his many affairs. Tomiko laughed, brushed his hands away from her, and went inside. He followed her. She was in a darkened closet off an interior hallway that led from the family room. Tsutomu pushed Tomiko against the wall with his body and embraced her. She shook her head left and right, and he grew irritated that she would not yield her lips to him. He grasped her face in his hands and pulled her close. She bit his upper lip.

Tsutomu had been mistaken. Not only did Tomiko not want him, she despised him because he was acting like every other man. She hated being handled roughly.

"Stop it! I don't want to! I won't be treated like this by you!"

Tsutomu came to his senses. A keen sadness penetrated his heart. He closed his eyes and, imagining that he was holding Michiko, gently hugged the body of the woman who was resisting him.

Just as Tomiko tried to put her arms around his neck, they heard someone coming through the garden. Akiyama's voice called out, "Tomiko!"

Tomiko went further inside and Tsutomu had no choice but to step out of the house.

"Tsutomu, it's been a while, hasn't it." Akiyama laughed sarcastically. "I just got home and heard you'd dropped by, so I decided to chase after you. Is your lip bleeding? Did the cat bite you?"

Tsutomu hastily wiped his mouth with the back of his hand.

"Where's Tomiko?" Akiyama peered inside.

"I don't know. Kitchen, maybe."

"That's convenient. There's something I want to talk about. That's why I came over here. It's about your feelings for Michiko."

Here was a sarcasm and barbed wit that Tsutomu had never heard from this academic. It was probably Tomiko's influence.

"That's something I'd like to have us talk about a little more seriously," Tsutomu said.

"How can I talk seriously about such a thing? Forgive the sentimental nuances, but Michiko is my wife after all."

"And she's my cousin too."

"Is that all she is to you? You were in a rather romantic situation the night of that storm. Ever since you two spent the night together in Murayama, I've been suffering from certain suspicions."

You're a liar, Tsutomu thought. Since Akiyama didn't care at all, this comment struck Tsutomu as strange. What was the purpose in suddenly bringing up the relationship between Michiko and him at this point? He could not fathom Akiyama's intent.

"If that's what you're worried about, you've got no choice but to believe the two of us," Tsutomu said. "Especially Michiko."

"If only I could believe you, everything would be fine. But you see, when push comes to shove..."

What did this "when push comes to shove" mean? Tomiko stepped out just then. She was laughing.

"Well if it isn't Mr. Akiyama. When did you get here? What are you two talking about so seriously?"

"We were just talking about the cut on Tsutomu's lip. I was asking if he hadn't been bitten by the cat."

"Really? Where is that cat? Oh, that looks terrible. You're bleeding. Let me put some antiseptic on it."

"Don't bother."

Akiyama wasn't jealous. A man involved with a coquette eventually has to dispense with that particular emotion. The reward is that the man can feel proud about his own magnanimity. And yet a lack of jealousy also reveals a carelessness that eventually becomes so much a part of the man's character that the one thing he cannot bear to lose is the woman who is the object of his magnanimity.

Akiyama was convinced that he was a fairly important man, but in fact he had fallen to a status as low as Ōno's. The money he gave to Tomiko was important to her, so he was convinced she would never leave him. He was in a position equal to her husband. Thus, he was able for the most part to ignore Tsutomu, who was nothing more than a poor college student.

Of the three of them, Tsutomu felt most embarrassed. He believed he had been rejected by Tomiko a few minutes earlier. His sense of inferiority was doubled when it appeared that Akiyama didn't really care all that much. In order to shake off his feeling of shame, he suggested that they take some photographs.

When Akiyama and Tomiko stood next to each other, Tsutomu sensed the same thing Michiko had sensed when she observed them facing the garden with their backs to her. He felt that he was being mocked.

Akiyama knew a little about cameras, so he graciously offered to take a picture of Tsutomu and Tomiko. Just as the shutter clicked, Tsutomu instinctively placed his arm on Tomiko's shoulder. Touched without warning, Tomiko's face was a little contorted when Akiyama snapped the photograph.

There was only a little film left. Akiyama said, "Let me develop this...as a memento." He quickly took some snapshots of the garden, as if he were firing a gun, and then removed the film.

Tsutomu shuddered at the thought that Michiko might see that photo of him with Tomiko. How would that defile their vow? It seemed to him that Akiyama had been waiting for such a chance, and had stolen the film. *Should I take it back by force? The film is already in his sleeve, so I'd have to make a scene to get it back. Never mind. I've already broken my promise by playing around with Tomiko. It's too late to even try to lie about it. It can't be helped. It took less than an hour for me to break the vow, so I would have betrayed Michiko eventually. Maybe it's best that she let me know early on that I'm not right for her.*

Tsutomu was convinced that it was over between him and Michiko, and he lost hope.

That photograph, however, had an effect entirely different from the one he predicted. The truth of the camera, showing the instant when Tsutomu placed his arm on Tomiko's shoulder, conveyed to Michiko nothing more than the ugliness of a paramour.

She sensed something completely different in the figures of her husband and Tomiko. She saw a kind of sorrow and unhappiness there.

Beginning with a discussion of how skillfully it was taken, people can glean various things from a photograph. The subject of a photograph often thinks the picture bears no resemblance to the way he or she really looks. Such a reaction is not necessarily because the photograph is in fact a poor likeness. It's just that many times a photograph doesn't reflect the person that the subject wants to be.

The meanings that Michiko took from these two photographs were inextricably bound up with the proposal Akiyama had made earlier in the evening, before he casually laid those pictures on the table and retreated to his study.

Chapter 12

A Reason for Divorce

Akiyama proposed a divorce.

"It's time we separated." Akiyama's face was like a mask as he spoke. "Monogamy is a fundamentally irrational system, you see. The only reason you and I have stayed together this long is that we're husband and wife in the eyes of the law. Now you've found someone you like in Tsutomu, and I...well, I'll go ahead and say it because I think you already know. I've fallen in love with Tomiko. She plans to divorce Ōno as well..."

Michiko, who was taken aback as she listened to him, finally broke in.

"She's planning no such thing."

"Whether she is or isn't, it's none of your business."

"It is my business! And what about Eiji?"

"It doesn't matter about him. Whatever you say, whatever you do, it makes no difference now. Our problems are more pressing. So what do you think? Can't we mutually agree to some rational settlement and not get too picky about convention?"

Michiko was completely at a loss. Her husband's words seemed to have fallen from the sky. She'd had a premonition that something like this might happen, but when he actually suggested the idea to her, she couldn't find a way to respond.

"It's all so sudden, I don't know what to say. I know I haven't been a perfect wife, but..."

"This has nothing to do with your imperfections. You did everything you could for me. It's just not human nature for people to spend their whole lives with one partner. With things as they are, you're unhappy and I'm unhappy. The best thing for us is to try to find happiness on our own."

"If you divorce me, do you really think that I'd find happiness at my age?"

"There's Tsutomu. He's a serious young man, and you truly love each other. I know very well how you've had to control yourself."

"It's not that kind of love."

"You protest too much. But I don't care. Since I proposed it, I'll take responsibility. And you decide your future on your own—the way you always do. The document that gives me power of attorney? I'll return it to you."

"Is that my consolation prize?"

"Don't use such a vulgar term. Think rationally. In places like America people can get a divorce very quickly when their marriage becomes meaningless. They
settle everything with an alimony payment. I won't give you alimony, but I'll hand over
this house, which is worth five hundred thousand yen. That should be plenty."

He forgot that he had obtained the right to dispose of the house by paying a
mere eighty thousand for the inheritance tax.

As she listened to her selfish husband's reasoning, Michiko gradually came
to believe that Akiyama was pathetic. She concluded that in the end everything was
due to his infatuation with Tomiko. But she also blamed herself for giving him the
excuse to turn his affections to another woman by being indifferent to him and silently passive as he became intimate with Tomiko. Her relationship with Tsutomu was
certainly another factor that had brought them to the point of talking about divorce.

Nonetheless, she could not suppress an idea that came to her in the midst
of all these considerations—the idea that, if they actually divorced, she could then be
together with Tsutomu. It never occurred to her that the opportunity to make their
vow a reality would come so soon. She was appalled by the very thought. After all,
wasn't it best to keep a vow within one's heart?

Divorce is such a serious matter that she was able put off her answer by asking for some time to think about it. Michiko had no confidante except Ōno, but he
was much too involved in the situation and she would not be able to confide everything to him. The professor who had once been Akiyama's adviser had also acted as
a go-between for their marriage. But his role had been mainly a formality, and the ob-
stinate Akiyama had not had much contact with him. Michiko suggested even so that
they talk to him, but Akiyama had no inclination to consult his old adviser. Michiko
was surprised when he demanded an answer within three days.

Akiyama had decided, after much consideration, that he would give up his
rights to the house. If he did not do that much for her, he would lose face in society.
He also reasoned that he had to resolve the matter quickly and decisively, even if it
meant making a sacrifice.

Michiko guessed that Tomiko would not be able to divorce Ōno so easily,
but she was wrong. Sex may not be necessary in keeping husbands and wives together,
but it is quite often a major cause of estrangement. If sex becomes unbearable for the
wife, and if she has someplace to go, then she will leave her husband.

Ōno's finances had been resolved to some extent, but the complications of
his sex life with Tomiko had not. His habit of forcing himself on his unwilling wife
had reached the stage where he took pleasure in the sheer exercise of his physical power. She could no longer put up with this. Quite apart from her affair with Akiyama,
Tomiko was now inclined to abandon her family.

Her parents were dead and her brothers had been killed in the war. So she decided that her destination would be her older sister's house in Osaka. She knew she would be stopped if she said anything beforehand, so to avoid complications she planned to run off without letting anyone know her plans.

The main problem was Yukiko. Tomiko was not, by nature, a woman who loved children, but if she ran away she would certainly feel sorry for her daughter. It was pathetic seeing how the generous-hearted Yukiko had studied the expressions on her parents' faces after Ōno had encountered his financial difficulties and the whole house had been thrown into turmoil.

One day Tomiko casually asked Yukiko the old question, "Who do you like better, Mama or Papa?" As always Yukiko answered, "Mama." However, she then added, as an afterthought, "But I don't like Uncle Akiyama." This caught Tomiko off guard.

"Why?"

"He reminds me of Kiuchi."

Kiuchi was a criminal who had kidnapped several young girls, causing a tremendous outcry in the city. One of the victims had gone to Yukiko's school, and for a time the maid had accompanied Yukiko to and from school as a precaution. Ōno had laughed about that. "Who's going to kidnap my kid? They'd never get a sen out of it." When the photograph of the criminal appeared in the paper, Yukiko thought it looked like Akiyama.

Now that she mentions it, Akiyama really is sly and dark, Tomiko thought, agreeing with her daughter. Even so, Tomiko did not think that the twenty-something criminal looked at all like Akiyama, whose hair was beginning to show flecks of gray. She concluded that Yukiko was probably unhappy at the prospect of having Akiyama around. Even Tomiko herself could not look at her lover's face without feeling a twinge of disgust.

It would be best to look after herself; and since it would not do to live idly at her sister's house, she planned to take up dressmaking or some such job. She had confidence in her own charms, and was sure that in the meantime something good would come her way. The reason Akiyama did not stand in the way of her goals was the geographical condition she set. She was planning to leave for the Kansai region, which he could not abide. This is why the question of divorce, which previously had come up only during their lovers' quarrels, became a reality.

One day, when Tomiko was complaining to Akiyama about her husband, she startled him by remarking, "Maybe I'll just walk out on Ōno and run off to my sister's place in Osaka." It had never occurred to him that Tomiko might act on her own. The money he had been giving her made him confident that their affair would continue.

"Oh really?" he said. "And what about me?"

"You've got Michiko, haven't you? Once I'm out of the picture you can live peacefully with her."

"You know perfectly well that without you around I couldn't live another day."

"Stop talking like a foreigner. When you have three meals to eat, the day flies by."

"Yes, and Christ also said that man does not live by bread alone...this isn't a joke. If you run away, I'll follow you to Osaka."

"That's just another one of your lies. You're always talking about leaving your house, but if you do, what happens to your job?"

"I'll quit. My monthly salary is for show. I can live off my translations."

"Don't say you'll do something you can't. You'll regret it."

"You think you can manage on your own? Without me?"

The tone of these last words was explicit. Tomiko grew sullen.

"Just leave me alone. Our relationship is hardly the romantic love you think it is. So what difference does it make what I do?"

With these words Tomiko unwittingly began to drive Akiyama out of his mind.

"I don't know when I'll leave," she finally told him. Her statement was nothing more than the capricious utterance of a coquette. But Akiyama took it seriously, and therefore broached the subject of divorce to Michiko and persisted in his demand for an answer from her.

Overcome by desire, he did not consider the difficulties presented by two couples getting divorced. Nor had he considered the difficulties of everyday life he would face once he and Tomiko were married. He thought it would all go smoothly, as easily as rearranging puppets.

Michiko received her three-day grace period, but she used the wiles she had learned as a wife and easily got the deadline extended to five days, then to a week, then to a fortnight. She believed everything depended on what Tomiko did.

Once he had said all he had to say, Akiyama withdrew to his study. On the day he first proposed a divorce, he had calculated the effect of the moment and nonchalantly tossed onto the table those two photographs, which he had been holding in reserve. "Tsutomu took these," he said to her. But the effect on Michiko was not at all what he had expected.

He was showing her the photographs to force her to consent to his affair with Tomiko. Michiko, however, detected in those figures only the sadness of a man and woman lost in illicit love. Her reaction was intimately connected to her awareness that she was to blame for Akiyama having fallen into such a state.

The effect on Michiko of the photograph of Tsutomu with his arm on Tomiko's shoulder was not at all what Akiyama and Tsutomu had expected. Akiyama's chronic jealousy had prompted him to steal the film from Tsutomu and show the pictures to Michiko. Showing them to her after suggesting that she could marry Tsutomu once they were divorced was a stimulus for him to abandon Michiko. It was the ultimate expression of a husband's cruelty against a powerless wife.

Michiko thought the photograph exhibited as unnatural a posture as the obscene pictures Akiyama had once forced her to look at—a man's arm reaching out, as in a dream, stretching from Tomiko's shoulder to her breast. Tomiko was looking diagonally down with a twisted, self-conscious smile. Michiko would never have believed the hand belonged to Tsutomu had his face not appeared in the picture beside Tomiko.

His face wore an expression Michiko had never seen before. His eyes, glancing toward the sky, seemed melancholy. They were the eyes of a man who had been overtaken by a dark impulse to do something he did not really want to do. They were just like the eyes of a criminal, and Michiko feared they resembled the eyes of Ogino Kenji, the robber from Hake who had been killed.

The photograph had been taken on the very day he had made his vow to her. She was shocked of course that he should have broken that vow so soon after he had left her.

Now, however, that fact was easier for her to bear. She herself had harbored doubts about the vow, though her doubts meant something different from Tsutomu's. If Tsutomu had not been able to keep his vow, then it had been a mistake to make it after all.

She was concerned about Tsutomu's criminal eyes. She truly believed that she had exercised her self-control not just for her own peace of mind, but for the sake of everyone at Hake. It was therefore painful for her to realize that she had shut out Tsutomu and driven him to such a dangerous position. She loved him, and so it never occurred to her that he ought to manage his problems by himself.

Looking at her own photograph, which Tsutomu had taken of her, she felt exactly the same way he did. She saw herself as an aging woman. She had always thought of herself that way, and wondered if that was how she was reflected in Tsutomu's eyes.

One reason Michiko postponed her response to her husband was that she believed, in light of her own feelings, that nothing really serious would happen between Tomiko and Akiyama so long as Tomiko was attracted to Tsutomu.

Then a crisis arose from an unexpected quarter. During an argument one evening, Tomiko hinted to Ōno that she might possibly leave for Osaka. Ōno began to plead with her, but she had already concluded that she no longer wanted to stay in his house, even if her husband were to be gentle. So she stated her intentions explicitly.

"What about Yukiko?" he said.

"I'll take her with me, of course. Do you think I'd leave her here with a man like you?"

Ōno realized that this time he would not be able to convince Tomiko to stay by himself, and so he went to Michiko for help. Michiko was struck by how his looks had deteriorated in such a short time. He had become slovenly, like a changed man. His athletic build had gone soft as a result of his drinking; his eyelids drooped, and his once large, bright eyes had narrowed like a toad's. Seeing his present condition, Michiko thought it was not at all unreasonable of Tomiko to be put off by him. She was tempted to feel sympathy for her rival in spite of herself.

Even so, Michiko was shocked to hear that Tomiko wanted to leave her home.

"I'm begging you to help," Ōno said. "She won't listen to me at all. Can't you talk to her for me?"

"She won't listen to me."

"At least you can talk to her as a woman, can't you?"

Ōno had no idea that the two women were, in one respect, like-minded, but it would never do to tell him that. She observed him closely. He was touched by her sad, sympathetic expression. Ever since his business had gone bad, Michiko was the only one who looked at him that way.

"Please do this for me," he said, suddenly embracing Michiko. She was startled and tried to shake herself loose, but could not free herself from Ōno's powerful arms.

"I should have married you," he said.

This possibility had in fact been considered at one time in the Miyaji house. They had both been students at the time, but Ōno, who loved brash things, chased after Tomiko and married her once his income was sufficient.

"What are you talking about? Let go, Eiji!"

But Ōno held onto her even more tightly. Michiko found this excruciatingly awkward. Then she began to feel the unhappiness of his compulsion to cling to her seep gradually into her body. She no longer felt the urge to resist.

As she impassively allowed Ōno to embrace her, Michiko suddenly realized that in her own way she was perhaps as much a coquette as Tomiko.

"Stop it. Let's go over to your house," she said, pushing at Ōno's chest.

Tomiko greeted them with fierce eyes. "Michiko has something she wants to talk to you about," Ōno said, retreating to another room. Michiko spoke as though she was trying to persuade a child. As she expected, Tomiko would not listen to her at all.

"I didn't want to marry Ōno. I said I didn't want to, but they practically forced me to come here."

"That's not how it was." Michiko stared at Tomiko's cold face. There was no way to talk to Tomiko, since she thought of Michiko as just another member of Ōno's family.

Michiko suddenly felt angry. Hadn't everything with Tsutomu and with Akiyama happened because this woman was here at Hake?

"What makes you think you have no responsibility?" she said.

"Responsibility? Why should an insignificant woman like me have to take responsibility when there are plenty of more respectable people around?"

"You mean that others ought to take responsibility, but you're free to do as you please?"

"You talk about responsibility, but everyone has their own way of handling it. Isn't putting up with a husband who is totally disgusting taking responsibility?"

"Ōno is putting up with you as well. That's what marriage is all about."

"Ōno puts up with me, but he also gets pleasure out of me. What do I get out of this?"

"Don't you get the pleasure of leading other men astray?"

Deeply insulted, Tomiko stood up.

"That's why I'm going to Osaka by myself. I'll be giving Akiyama back to you, so don't worry too much. Isn't that why you came here, to ask me to give him back?"

"You're cruel." Michiko lowered her head as she spoke.

Ōno resorted to an underhanded trick by directly contacting Tomiko's older sister in Osaka for help. Her sister had married the owner of a small steelworks in Amagasaki, and they had three children together. She ran a peaceful household, and enjoyed the troubles of others.

She came to Tokyo as soon as Ōno invited her. She arrived while he was out, barged right in from the veranda, and leaned her large-framed body against the wall. "What do you think you're doing?" she blurted out. "You've been married ten years and now you say you want a divorce? Is there anything more idiotic?"

Like Tomiko, she had been born in Tokyo, but to give a lighter tone to her speech she affected a bad Osaka accent.

"You're not behaving well, Tomi-chan," she said. "There's absolutely no reason you can't put up with things in your own home."

"This time I'm serious," said Tomiko.

She then proceeded to relate all the intimate details of her sex life with Ōno, which she had found so hard to endure. Her sister laughed. Speaking in a Tokyo accent now, she said, "You're so stupid. Just be quiet and do whatever your husband says, and it'll be fine. If you go along with them, men get tired of things really quickly. Then you won't have to do anything at all and you'll be able to live as comfortably as you please. There aren't many good men like Ōno out there."

When Ōno got back that evening, the sister spoke to him. "Just because your bride is complaining and threatening to leave, there's no reason for you to get all flustered and make a big fuss about it. Once your business gets back on track, everything will go back to the way it was."

"Tomiko says the same thing. I'll let it go for now, but next time it's over."

She laughed and said, "You mustn't let your wife see through you. A man has to keep some things hidden from a woman."

As a diversion she took Tomiko and Yukiko into Tokyo for a few days, and they went to the movies and the theater. When the older sister left to go back to Osaka, she made a point of saying to Tomiko, "You may still be planning to sneak away at some point, but you are forbidden to come to my house. Don't even think that's a possibility for you."

By placing her house off limits to Tomiko, she thought she would be able to force her to stay with Ōno. As it turned out, she was wrong.

An eminent Russian writer once remarked that the all happy families are alike, but each unhappy family is unhappy in its own way . Tomiko's sister drew her analogies from her own happy family; but what held true for most families was not applicable to others.

Tomiko's capacity to feel strong hatred was in equal proportion to her weakness for pleasure, and that was the source of her unhappiness.

Her hatred eventually exploded, and led Akiyama and Michiko to a disaster that had distinctly different consequences for each of them.

CHAPTER 13

AUTUMN

One evening in November, ten days after Tomiko's sister had returned to Osaka, Ōno came home from the factory to find the interior of the house unusually tidy. This tidiness struck him as odd. Yukiko and the old woman who helped them out were sitting blankly at the dinner table.

"Mama's gone," Yukiko said.

"Running errands in Tokyo?"

Yukiko's face suddenly contorted. "I don't know what she's doing. Last night when I went to bed, she said good-bye."

"I see." Ōno still didn't get it. He spotted a letter on a desk that had been placed in one of the inner rooms for show. "To my husband" was written on the envelope. It wasn't sealed. He read the letter inside.

I will definitely come for Yukiko. Until then please do not look for me. Thank you for all you did for me. I just cannot continue living with you.

Ōno had been having premonitions about this. He immediately sent a telegram to Tomiko's sister in Osaka: *Tomiko arrives tomorrow a.m. Will leave it to you. Upon arrival, send telegram.*

On the way back from the post office he dropped by Michiko's house and learned that Akiyama was away. For the first time he grew uneasy.

Michiko looked worn and thin. She had managed to put off both Akiyama's demands for a divorce and his three-day time limit. However, she had grown weary listening to his reasons for wanting a divorce, which he persistently repeated night after night. His rationale was always the same—when one of the partners in a loveless marriage finds someone else, the most sensible way to deal with the situation is divorce.

"Look at America," Akiyama would say. "Even Charlie Chaplin has been divorced five or six times."

"You always hated America. Didn't you say it was far too rational?"

"In this case, America has it right. Since the war ended, divorce is becoming more common even in Japan. Most Japanese are negligent and lax about making support payments when they do get divorced, but I won't be like that. I plan to pay everything in one lump sum."

"It's never been a question of money. Why can't you see what it means for a woman to be divorced by a man she's lived with for ten years?"

"You're too old-fashioned. I don't think you take our relationship all that seriously. The sanctity of marriage is a foreign concept. In ancient Japan it used to be that a wife could leave a household rather easily, depending on her needs. You're deceiving yourself about this."

"I'm not deceiving anyone. I'm thinking about you. If you leave this house, where will you live?"

"An apartment somewhere. You just have to pay enough to get in."

"You have that kind of money?"

Akiyama's income consisted of his monthly salary from the college and the supplement provided by his royalties. Recently he had used some of his money to pay for his trysts with Tomiko, so he began to give the income from his royalties to Michiko later and later. A wife is the first to know if her husband is struggling to raise money.

Money, in fact, was Akiyama's weak point. The boom time for postwar publishing had passed its peak, and though his translations of Stendhal were still selling, the royalties from his publishers were not as good as they had been.

"I won't rely on your help." As soon as he said this, Michiko detected in his glare a flash like the eyes of a beast, a light she'd never seen before in her husband. She wondered, *Have I really lived with this man for ten years?*

They repeated this conversation every night, and during that time Michiko came to believe there was some unshatterable core in Akiyama's heart. She could rely only on the wisdom she had gained from her experience as a wife, and so that core would inevitably defeat her in the end. There was something fantastic, something dreamlike to her about Akiyama's determination to destroy his home for the sake of an affair with Tomiko. She brooded so much over her husband's feelings because she was inexperienced. She thought that she had to be steady and firm from now on.

In the end she told him, "I'll never agree to your request."

The day Ōno dropped by her house Akiyama was out. He had left, saying that he was taking a short trip around the southern part of the Izu peninsula to get away for a few days in order to proofread the manuscript of a translation. Michiko was surprised to hear from Ōno that Tomiko had run off. She had been inclined to put her trust in the capricious Tomiko.

"Is it true?" she muttered.

"I think she went to Osaka."

"You're probably right about that. Akiyama's on a trip, but..." She wanted to add, *They wouldn't have gone together, would they?* The same thought had occurred to Ōno, but he could not bring himself to say it.

"Anyway, why don't you wait for an answer from Osaka?" Michiko said. "Her sister will take care of things for you. This must be hard on you, Eiji. Whatever happens, Yukiko can stay with me for a while."

"I appreciate your help, but it probably won't come to that. Things will turn out one way or another. I'll probably have to take Yukiko with me to Osaka."

Neither of them knew that Tomiko's sister had made it clear that, no matter what, Tomiko would not be allowed to stay at the house in Osaka.

Even while he was arguing every night with Michiko about getting a divorce, Akiyama was demanding that Tomiko marry him. After being taunted by Tomiko about his inability to get a divorce, he became obsessed with the notion of abandoning his home. At the same time, if he wanted to hold onto Tomiko's heart, then he had no other recourse but to propose marriage. Yet for Tomiko, running away from her home and continuing her affair with Akiyama were not necessarily connected.

"I can't stand having to do something that's beyond my ability," Tomiko said. "A timid dawdler like you could never divorce Michiko. Even I feel sorry for her."

A woman who could say such a thing would not consider it unreasonable to abandon her husband and child.

Her words further inflamed Akiyama's emotions. When she said she did not feel like going to Osaka, even if she left Ōno, he became consumed with the dream of living with her in Tokyo. The difficulty was scraping together enough to pay the key money and deposit for a place that wasn't run-down. Of the three publishers who had published his translations, two of them had gone under already. For two or three days he desperately went around trying to raise money, but he failed to get what he needed, and was nearly beside himself.

The time for Tomiko's escape was drawing near. Her plan was to come up with some way to support herself temporarily—by dressmaking or whatever else she could find. But deep in her heart she figured that, if she began to struggle, her relatives would not cut her loose because they would want to maintain at least the facade of family dignity. For now, as part of her contingency plan, she preferred to continue receiving help from Akiyama.

Tomiko discussed her future with Akiyama at the inn in Shinjuku where they always met. He arrived there in the evening after telling Michiko he was going on his trip. Michiko, who had been warned by Ōno's news that Tomiko had fled, decided to investigate her husband's study. She discovered that two documents were missing from the files: the document granting Akiyama power of attorney to transfer the title of the house at Hake, and the title deed.

The document that laid out the terms of the agreement on the power of attorney was the one Akiyama had said he would give Michiko as a divorce settlement. Michiko's belief that her husband could never abandon her was based on the knowledge that he did not have enough money to afford a divorce. These missing documents were thus decisive proof that he had decided to leave her. For the first time Michiko began to wonder if she had done the right thing by denying him a divorce to the bitter end.

She recalled what her husband had said to her: "If you don't listen to me and grant me a divorce, there's no telling what I'll do."

It was her willfulness that had led her, after she married, to defend Akiyama against her father and brother, who affected the mannerisms of the old samurai class. It was the queen bee instinct of an heiress, following the deaths of her parents and brothers, that allowed her to pretend not to notice her husband's affair. Now that she had lost her estate, there was no longer any reason for her to live.

Tsutomu was the only one left, but he was an unprincipled young man who could not keep a vow for even two hours. Now that she had been cast aside by Akiyama, the chance to realize her vow was at hand. But even if everything worked out, she was five years older than Tsutomu and had no property. She was therefore convinced that he would never be able to keep their vow. *None of it matters*, she thought, *since Tsutomu has probably forgotten about me by now.* Two or three days earlier she had mailed the photograph of him and Tomiko to his apartment. She sent no letter with it.

Michiko thought that everything was finished for her.

A November rain fell all through the night. It struck the eaves, dripping on all sides from the cracked gutters and producing a concert of uncanny noises that enclosed the old house.

Michiko walked by herself from room to room. The familiar walls and ceilings, the furnishings that displayed her father's tastes, were all damp, dark, and disgusting to her. She had a feeling that she had experienced these same sensations long ago. It occurred to her that ever since her childhood she had persisted like a low-pitched note in the depths of her own life, which she had considered to be happy and to lack for nothing. Now, as the years passed, even the rational design of her father's life came to seem stagnant and decayed.

Her father had been an atheist, and so he had never installed a Buddhist altar in the house. When she wanted to recall her father lovingly, she would sit at the rosewood table he used when he was alive. This was the same desk Akiyama used for writing letters and such. Now that he had left, memories came drifting back to Michiko as she sat at the desk. She had stopped loving him long ago, but at least he was someone she protected as part of the household at Hake. He had made his way honorably in society as a scholar, and he had given to her the title most becoming to a woman of her age—the title of *wife*. She realized, now that he was gone, just how accustomed she had grown to the ease conferred by that title.

Hereafter she would go by the designation of *abandoned wife*. It would be difficult to endure such wretchedness. It made her angry to think of her state as wretched. She felt that somehow she had to break the spell that held her.

She had no regrets over the title deed that Akiyama had taken. She looked on it as compensation to him for supporting her for ten years, as well as for paying the estate tax. Indeed, it made her feel more comfortable to give it to him. What she found hard to forgive was his decision to dispose of the house as the means to run off with another woman.

The lawyer who drew up the document granting power of attorney to Akiyama had laughed about it. He said, "This document means that it will be easier to transfer ownership. I'm sure you've agreed to this on the assumption that your husband will not use the power selfishly. But you really ought to hold on to the title deed, because the house can only be sold when these two documents are together."

"If the wife dies, the power of attorney is still in force, isn't it?" Akiyama asked.

"No, it would no longer be in force. But you'd inherit the estate then, wouldn't you?"

Akiyama's words, "If the wife dies," had stung Michiko. She examined a legal commentary that summarized the new civil code, and learned that if she made a will, she could give two thirds of her estate to whomever she wanted.

Akiyama had taken both documents, obviously relying on what the lawyer had said. Michiko figured that the only way for her to block the sale of the house was to die. And she had to die before he sold it.

Both Michiko and Akiyama assumed that the sale of a property could be carried out easily. Their assumptions showed just how ignorant of the world they truly were.

Should she die right away? Would she really be able to die? Listening to the sound of the rain enveloping the house, now far, now near, she passed the night lost in thought. When a late November morning at last shone brightly on the panes of glass in the hallway, Michiko decided she should write her will. The gist of it was simple. Excluding the portion that would go to Akiyama as the legal heir, she gave half of the remaining portion to Tsutomu and half to Ōno. That was all there was to it. Michiko, whose mind was completely turned toward death, thought, *Even when I'm dead this testament will settle the matter of the land Ōno used for security, and no one will be hounded by Akiyama.*

Michiko was afraid that her will would fall into Akiyama's hands and be discarded. She decided to walk over to Ōno's house and leave it with him. The road that morning was still wet from the rain.

Ōno was waiting for a telegram from Osaka, and so he decided not to go to work until after it arrived. Michiko now realized that Tomiko had not gone to Osaka, but she thought she shouldn't say anything. If she killed herself, Akiyama would never be able to show himself in public with Tomiko. In that case, Tomiko would eventually return to Ōno. It seemed that everything would come to an amicable conclusion if she killed herself. Michiko felt she was being driven more and more in the direction of death.

Yukiko was being difficult, saying she would not go to school until her mother came home. Michiko cajoled her and got her to go to school by saying, "Your mother will be sure to come home while you're away." After Yukiko left, Michiko set the will down in front of Ōno.

"I've been thinking of leaving this with you for some time, " she said. "If I should die, please read it."

"This is rather sudden, isn't it? Shouldn't you be giving it to Akiyama?"

"I can't give it to him. I have to give it to someone else."

"All right, if you say so. But it's a little strange."

Michiko had not slept all night, and Ōno had been disconcerted by her odd appearance from the moment she showed up.

"Something's wrong," he said. "You look really pale."

"You don't look well yourself. Are you worried about Tomiko?"

"She's beyond worrying about. Her family indulged her too much."

"You're the one who indulged her."

"Maybe you're right. But haven't you pampered Akiyama?"

"I didn't spoil him. He's always been selfish."

"So has Tomiko. I feel sorry for Yukiko."

"So do I."

Michiko, who was childless, loved Yukiko. It suddenly struck her that if Akiyama and Tomiko were together, she could move to Ōno's place, as Ōno had once suggested. Perhaps things would calm down if everyone could get to a point where they could compose themselves. She quickly squelched the thought. What could possibly be more pathetic than two abandoned spouses living together?

"Can you look after Tsutomu?" she asked.

"You mean have him to come work for me when he graduates? I'm not so well off now, and wouldn't be able to help him much. I could introduce him around, but Tsutomu doesn't strike me as the type who wants to be a salaried employee."

"That's precisely why you have to get him into a respectable place."

"There aren't many respectable places these days. You can barely live on a monthly wage as it is."

"Things are settling down a bit, aren't they?"

"Settling down? Just look at us." Ōno was mocking himself.

He still thought Michiko was behaving strangely, especially the way she combined her concern for Tsutomu with the business of her will. The old woman who was helping him out was going tomorrow to get the rations for his house, and it helped set Ōno's mind at ease to hear Michiko ask the old woman to pick up her rations as well. Even so, he was startled again by the intensity with which Michiko's lonely face stared at him when she left. He reminded himself that she had asked that her rations be picked up the next day, and so was rather unreasonably persuaded that nothing would happen at least until tomorrow. He was just too preoccupied with his worries about Tomiko.

The telegram from Osaka was slow in coming. If Tomiko had gone there, she would have arrived by morning. An urgent telegram should have been delivered by now. In his mind he went back over the message he'd sent yesterday, and realized that if Tomiko had not shown up, then it was entirely possible her easygoing sister might assume that no reply was necessary. He went to the post office again and sent a revised message: *Has Tomiko arrived or not? Waiting for reply.*

Michiko hurried toward the Tama Cemetery, which was across the Nogawa from Ōno's house, to visit the place where the spirits of her parents and brothers slept. She had not definitely made up her mind to commit suicide. People are not capable of deciding on such an action in advance. Most people have a motive for suicide, and often they make a genuine resolution to go through with it. But actually committing suicide depends, for the most part, upon the contingencies of the moment.

The trees in Tama Cemetery had turned. Musashino is about fifty meters above sea level in this area, and the first frost of the season normally occurs at the beginning of November. Then, as a sign that autumn has arrived, the leaves on the deciduous trees—Japanese maples, sumac, birches—all change colors in a blaze.

In the late 1920s town officials in Tama came up with the idea of selling off the low-priced pine lands in the vicinity and putting in a graveyard to handle the increasing number of dead from Tokyo. Recognizing that it was appropriate to landscape the place in a fashion more cheerful than the old Meiji period cemeteries in Yanaka and Aoyama, they designed the cemetery with radial roads and tree-lined paths. Many notable families bought up the wide plots that faced the main roads, and decorated them with Western-style stone structures and bronze statues.

Of course Michiko's father sneered at all this. "What a bunch of pretentious fools. Do they really think their reputations will stay around as long as stone and metal?"

For the sake of economizing he purchased a small plot for his wife and himself on an obscure side road. The stone marker was modest, but he had various trees and shrubs—Japanese quince, camellia, crape myrtle, sweet osmanthus, gingko, azalea—planted around it. They colored each of the seasons in their own way. Placed so closely together on this narrow plot, their dense shapes were already crowding over into the neighboring plots.

Japanese maples, which the cemetery's planners had set out almost indiscriminately, filled the surroundings with a lovely crimson. The azaleas surrounding the Miyaji plot had sunk the red of their leaves, which were just like flowers, into the depths of the clear autumn sky. The forms of nature in the process of dying seeped comfortingly into Michiko's eyes.

She squatted before the stone marker on which the name "Miyaji" was carved. Lifting the flat stones in front of the marker, she revealed a recess underneath. A shelf had been constructed on the façade to hold the funeral urns.

When they placed her mother's remains here, her father had withdrawn inside himself. He said, "What a nice feeling. I'd like to come to such a place soon." How much better would it be to join her mother, father, and brothers than to continue her daily suffering?

Even as she was absorbed in these thoughts, she clung to the possibility of living with Ōno, which she had imagined earlier when she sent Yukiko off to school. She neither liked nor disliked Ōno, but she could be a substitute mother for poor Yukiko. Life is trying to live to the fullest. Where there is no way to live, life will project fantasies into the future.

"What should I do, father?"

The gravestone was silent. She remembered that her father, the son of a samurai, had been proud of the steely attitude he brought to questions of life and death. "When I was a child, there were still Japanese who committed *seppuku*," he had said. "Christianity proscribed suicide because if slaves continued to kill themselves their masters would suffer losses. Confucianism has no such sodden notions. When there is a purpose to death, you kill yourself. This is the action of a noble person. *Seppuku* is, for our nation, the proper conclusion of Confucian teaching."

Muttering the word "action," Michiko suddenly revised her thinking. *That's right. I have to stop Akiyama from disposing of the house as he wishes.* Her lingering attachment to Ōno and Yukiko was a mistake.

The vision of living happily with Tsutomu floated before her again. She dispelled that vision as well. *If I lived with him, I'd fall into the same brutish condition as Akiyama and Tomiko. Besides, Tsutomu is the kind of young man who can put his arm across the shoulder of a woman like Tomiko. That's right, isn't it? If I leave him my estate, perhaps he'll come to understand. It's best for me to die.* With that, Michiko made her decision and left her father's grave.

The natural world of autumn in the cemetery was transformed. She felt as though nature was pressing in on her, burning with the single color of red. Her eyes saw almost nothing.

At that very moment Tsutomu was standing at the edge of one of the three outcroppings on the heights at Sayama. He had come here to take in the view of Musashino. He had missed this view when he visited with Michiko at the end of the summer, because they had gone straight to the reservoir. No doubt the real purpose in his heart was to experience a place that held memories of Michiko.

Tsutomu was constantly thinking of her. She sent the photograph of him and Tomiko, but did not include a letter. He took that as proof that he had completely lost favor. In his eyes the figure he cut in the picture was extremely ugly. *I act according to an inner force, but if I present such an ugly outward appearance...well, I'm not sure, but just maybe the things inside me that I assume are right aren't right after all.*

The photograph he had taken of Michiko, which had been included with the photograph of him and Tomiko, struck him as beautiful in comparison. This was the photograph that had made him think, as he peered through the viewfinder, that she looked like an old woman. It had made Michiko aware of her age as well. Her face, squinting in the glare as she gazed into the lens, was filled with a sorrow and grief she was probably unaware of herself. Tsutomu thought, *She's inflicted a burden on herself she can't bear. Is there something wrong with me to think I wanted to take her away from the house at Hake? That place isn't right for her at all. But I can't do anything in a way that would satisfy her. And the vow? Was I wrong to be so weak, to be so willing to break it? If in fact I was so inclined, then what could I do about it? If I were truly good, then the vow would have been a mistake. If I hadn't heard it from her lips, I probably would never have accepted such a thing. Because a vow is nothing more than a weak person's refusal to admit defeat. What I hate about all this is that Akiyama is the one who made her think such a thing.* He hated all husbands, for whom Akiyama was the archetype. He hated society.

Lost in these dark thoughts, Tsutomu gazed deep into Musashino. The promontory where he was standing looked out over an ancient battleground of the Kamakura period. Because the generals of both armies rose up and joined the fray, a stele with the inscription "Mound of the Generals" had been erected here. From this vantage he should have been able to see the length and breadth of the Musashino plateau, which spanned about twenty-four kilometers each way. However, the only things visible from this outcropping, which was about thirty meters high from its base, were woods and paddies stretching about a kilometer from Tokorozawa to Akitsu and Kumegawa. Tsutomu's topographical illusion was shattered.

The woods and paddies displayed their beautiful autumn attire. Among all the deciduous trees turning colors, some thin-topped zelkova stood in a line, looking as though they were sweeping the sky. *Kitateha* butterflies, their yellow wings standing erect, swarmed in persimmon trees filled with ripened fruit. Slender, drooping bamboo, tinged a faint yellow, swayed gently in the breeze. Racks of upland rice had been placed at intervals, almost as if they were abandoned, between long rows of tea plants that appeared a shade blacker in contrast to the crimson and yellow all around them.

The deep azure sky of autumn was filled with the roar of a plane that left a trail as it flew off on exercises somewhere. Its vapor trail carved a great white circle high above. Puffed up by a wind blowing from the north at the upper altitudes, the circle slowly began moving south.

Tsutomu set off. The trees began to thin out along the path that hugged the ridgeline extending from the Mound of the Generals to the Murayama Reservoir. Low thickets covered the sides of the path as far down as the base of the ridge.

Here and there the hard flowers of sasanqua emerged unexpectedly from among the sumac and lacquer trees, which were showing off their conspicuous foliage.

Tsutomu was no longer thinking about Michiko. He was thinking about society. More precisely, he was thinking about how society had hindered his love for Michiko.

The suburban train line that carried him here from Tokyo had stations near many of the schools that dotted the broad plain of Musashino. Students, with their dirty clothes, were sitting in waiting areas, or reading books, or turning vacant stares to the trains that were arriving and departing. Passing through the various stations on his way, Tsutomu got a strange feeling each time he saw students like this.

They all had the same social status as he. They were poor and weary. Many of them believed in Marxism. These students justified their weariness as a necessity. They seemed comical to him. They reasoned that the war had also been a necessity. But Tsutomu, who had experienced the reality of war, knew that in war there was a madness and a disorder that cannot be gauged by the word *necessity*.

Could he explain his love for Michiko on the basis of necessity? There were many things about the actions people took that could not be judged on such a basis. So, wasn't it a mistake to insist on necessity as an explanation? He could see nothing but madness behind the necessity these students invoked.

If we are creatures whose lives are not controlled by necessity, then I ought to be able to proclaim my love just as these people proclaim the idea of necessity. That's why it shouldn't matter if I turn my back on that part of society formed out of necessity.

Tsutomu, an ex-soldier, thought nothing of breaking the conventions of society. Yet by the same token he could not force Michiko, who had rejected him because she was bound by convention, to be his lover.

The roar of the plane, like the droning of bees, still echoed in his ears. The circular vapor trail that had been moving south was now broken into two semicircles. Curling into two large hooks, they collapsed to a comma shape, moving slowly to the southwest and the skies over Tokyo.

The movement of that vapor trail transcends necessity. For me there is only love.

He came to the embankment of the reservoir where he had once stood with Michiko. The trees on the shore had lost their green color, and so had the water. It was now a muddy, cobalt blue. It was also calm this time. Grebes flocked near the center of the lake, thrusting their heads into the water now and then, flapping their wings, gliding across the surface, and taking off into the air. There was the toy-like water tower. Tsutomu imagined the water, which was drawn up from the lower part of the tower, passing through the aqueducts that crisscrossed the wide Musashino plateau, going through the water treatment plants, dividing into countless narrower water mains, and ending up in the myriad homes of Tokyo.

Tsutomu thought that if he dumped poison into this tower, he might be able to kill all the citizens of Tokyo at a single stroke. His own thought shocked him.

He had never anticipated that he would have this kind of fantasy. He had absolutely no interest in the necessity that guided the people of Tokyo, who were living on the alluvial soil about twenty-four kilometers from here. So why did he have to think that it might actually feel good to kill those people with poison? Seeing that his idea of turning away from necessity led him to atrocious fantasies, he became afraid of himself.

Depressed, he descended the embankment, which now held these unpleasant associations for him. The row of cherry trees he and Michiko had once walked past had lost all their leaves and now spread their black branches against the sky. His feet, almost of their own accord, turned in the direction of Kokubunji, toward Hake.

He followed the same road he and Michiko had taken the morning after the typhoon. Islands of trees drifted on the flat landscape among the rice paddies of Musashino, each with its own changing colors. Stark rows of black alders on the levees that divided the rice paddies struck ominous poses. In the drainage ditches along the roadside, where muddy water had flowed after the storm, the volume of the runoff had decreased, the current was gentler, and, since the mud and silt had sunk to the bottom, the water was clear. The surface of the blue water reflected the withered grasses on the banks and glowed with a faint yellowish tinge.

He could not shake the fantasy that had come to him at the water tower. *Am I that evil? If the sum of all I experienced in Burma as a soldier in a defeated army comes to this, how can I remain in the presence of human beings? Michiko was right not to be my lover. That photograph she sent me shows the face of a brute. And it's not just my face. My heart is not human.*

He felt like some convicted criminal who bore the brand VETERAN on his forehead.

He once thought he had been lucky to have been able to pick up with his life and come home. *It would have been better if I had died over there. That's the truth. If I had died, I would never have felt this kind of guilt.*

It was easy to die in the chaos of the jungle. If I think that I died back then, what regrets could I have about dying now?

Should I die with Michiko? There's another selfish, evil thought. What reason would she have to die? Do I want to murder her as well?

In the distance he could see Mt. Fuji under clouds dyed copper by the evening sun. The mountain already wore a full crown of snow, and the dark remains of the lava flow around the peak lay exposed.

This elegant conical volcano, which previously reflected back an image of unchanging love to Tsutomu, now suggested death to him.

It has such a symmetrical cone because it's still a young volcano. After it has passed through a geological age, it'll be worn down and small. It'll end up as a craggy mountain, ugly as a crab crawling along. Tsutomu took no pleasure in these thoughts.

What the hell. I won't be around when Fuji starts to look like a crab. What good are these fantasies to me? For the first time since he had been demobilized he was harboring serious doubts about his life. *Isn't my obsession with topography just an emotional delusion?*

I could never view the Musashino plateau, even though I climbed Sayama several times. So that's just a fantasy as well, isn't it? What does the delta of the ancient Tamagawa have to do with me? That river existed long before I was born. Even the forests of Musashino that people talk about so much? Weren't they all planted just to protect generations of peasants from the wind? Factories, schools, airports, the sprawling residences of the citizens of Tokyo. These things are Musashino now.

As he went along, shattering his delusions about the topography of Musashino, Tsutomu, almost without realizing it, shattered his fantasies about death as well. *If even someone like me wants to go on living, come what may, then I'll have to make a new beginning.*

His heart turned again to Michiko. *Perhaps there's some meaning in that absurd vow. If society can't change, then perhaps I can find a way to live by figuring out the inclinations of my own heart. If that's the only path left to me, then it can't be helped.*

Michiko turned her back on me all because of my own foolish behavior. But it isn't too late to change. From now on I'll have to see if I can keep that vow.

The trees grew denser as he neared Hake. They were at the peak of their color. This was the first autumn in Japan he had seen in four years. He had spent the previous autumns looking at the lush greens of Burma. It was uncanny that a feeling of rapture should rise up within him as he walked through a world in the process of dying.

Someone appeared from a side road and was walking in front of him. He wasn't alone.

All right, I'll try going in through the back garden of the house and see if she's there. I promised I wouldn't come here until she called me, but what difference does it make, so long as she doesn't know I'm here?

He planned to hop over the hedge if the door was locked, but to his surprise the door opened when he pushed on it. *This is strange. I wonder what happened? It was locked last time. I'll have to check it out later.*

He went into the thicket of yellow roses above the spring of Hake, where he had crouched that June afternoon. The yellow roses, having dropped their leaves, stretched out their rod-like stalks. If he did not lie prostrate, he would not be able to hide.

Michiko was on the veranda. She was dressed in an unusual fashion, in fine clothing of ancient crepe silk. He assumed she was going out somewhere.

In the autumn the flow of water from the spring at Hake declined, and because it just barely filled the bamboo conduit that drew water into the kitchen, the murmuring of the water was low. The magpies had left the treetops, and only the voices of thrush and bulbul echoed.

As she had in June, Michiko was sitting with her back toward him. The shape of her ears was familiar, and a flood of memories of their intimacy during the brief interlude when he had lived at Hake swept over him. *Is it foolish to think, as I'm watching her like this, that it's wrong to call out to her? I know it's forbidden for me to come here, but if I just showed myself, she wouldn't flatly reject me, would she?*

But then there's the vow. If I go down there now, the vow would be meaningless. And that's something worth living for. I've already given in to my impulses once, so if I just shamelessly show up, she'll despise me. I've got to hold on.

If I talk to her about it later, she'll probably praise me. She praised me that time I restrained myself at the hotel in Murayama. That's right, isn't it? At least there's that much goodness in me.

Michiko was putting what looked like white pills into a glass. It seemed like a lot to him. Apparently she poured seltzer in as well, because there was so much foam and the drink was cloudy white. She stirred and drank the mixture, which he assumed was some sort of medicine.

She stood up and turned in his direction. She was looking straight at the thicket where Tsutomu was hiding. He thought her eyes were overflowing with the love he had seen there so many times. *This is really odd. Does she know I'm here? She can't know.* He shrank down even further.

She did not know he was there. She was looking not at his face, but at a clump of withered yellow roses just a little above him. Her face was gaunt with anguish, but to Tsutomu, who was in torment himself, she did not look gaunt at all.

Michiko was gazing for the last time at the area above the spring where Tsutomu had appeared once before. She had gone out of her way to unlock the back gate after she decided to die and leave her estate to Tsutomu.

Unable to bear the sight of Michiko's love, he thought he ought to rustle the thicket as a sign of his presence, just as he had that earlier time. But he managed to control himself.

If he had been quick-witted enough to guess what kind of medicine Michiko had dissolved in the seltzer water just now, he would have gone down to her at once in spite of their vow. Had he done so, there might have been a chance for him and Michiko to have experienced a happiness they never expected to have, however ephemeral that happiness might have been.

Or perhaps they would have died together—an idea that had flashed across his heart once.

As it was, he hurriedly left the garden so that he would not be overcome by her gaze. Fate follows an inevitable path for each person. It never ceases to weave the drama of humanity.

The tablets Michiko mixed with seltzer in that glass were the sleeping pills Akiyama had obtained at the end of the war, when rumors flew that the American army would land at the nearby airfield. He gave them to her saying, "I'll never use these."

Chapter 14

The Heart

When Tomiko woke up that morning, she was momentarily taken with the illusion that she was in the bedroom of her house in Hake. She needed to get Yukiko ready to go off to school. But everything was different. The ceiling, the shoji screens. It was a room at the inn in Shinjuku where she always met Akiyama. This was the first time she ever woke up here. They had never stayed over before.

Akiyama was snoring. His wrinkles and the gray beginning to streak his hair stood out in the light of dawn. His nostrils looked absurdly large.

He woke up at the signs of morning, and exchanged glances with Tomiko. He made a blank, disinterested face, but then, as if reconsidering, smiled flirtatiously. He drew near to give her a kiss and asked, "What are you thinking?"

Tomiko hated that question, which he was always putting to her. She never liked anyone asking her what she was thinking. She didn't want to say, and if she had let the questioner know what she was thinking, he would have plenty to feel sorry about.

"I wonder...." She just smiled back at him.

The time she had passed the night before talking with Akiyama weighed heavily on her mind. It was certainly better than time spent at home fighting with Ōno, but it was a bother to have to come up with some topic of conversation all the time. She could not avoid telling him her plans for the future, but the more they discussed their plans in detail, the more their talk struck her as delusional and foolish.

Akiyama had managed to scrape together a little cash from his publisher, but he had done nothing about the transfer of the title of the house at Hake. She was not satisfied about that.

"Taking care of that is the most important thing, isn't it?" she said.

"Of course it is. I just didn't feel like meeting with all those people yesterday. I wanted to be with you. I'm worn out."

"We're just starting out, and you're already exhausted? That's odd. But it doesn't matter to me. I don't plan to count on you anyway."

"That's a terrible thing to say to me. Haven't I been doing all this for you?"

"It has nothing to do with me...I don't care one way or the other. Now that you mention it, maybe I'm worn out too."

She had left her house around three and come straight to the inn, where she'd had nothing to do but wait for Akiyama.

"Look," he said, "I couldn't get that much from the publisher, so I plan to get moving on things tomorrow morning."

"Shouldn't you get help from a lawyer or an accountant?"

"They'll just ask a lot of troublesome questions. At this point it's better to deal with a real estate company that can handle this under-the-counter. They can take care of things right away."

The truth was that Akiyama was afraid to dispose of the house. His intentions were not as bad as Michiko had imagined. If he sold the place for four hundred thousand yen, he would be able to take a lease on a smaller house for about one hundred thousand and live with Tomiko there. He would then give the remainder to Michiko. Once Michiko was on her own, the house at Hake would be too big for her. And in any case the land was mortgaged, so the house was already lost. Thinking things over in this self-serving manner, he had put off selling the place for a day.

He said, "Shall we go out this morning?" But in the end they lazed about until after ten o'clock.

"You can stay here and relax, if you want," Akiyama said.

"I suppose I could," said Tomiko. "But I'm bored. Maybe I'll go see a movie."

"All right, then, shall we meet around four in the Ginza somewhere?"

For several days Akiyama had been considering going to a real estate company in Kanda. The office, which was located in a newly constructed barracks, consisted of a few cheap tables and chairs in a room partitioned by screens. The young man who came out to receive him was far better dressed than he was. After asking Akiyama about his occupation and age, he said, "Excuse me, but could you tell me why you're selling the house?"

"The location is inconvenient," Akiyama said. "I've been thinking about buying a place that's a little closer to work."

"So you're saying that you want to sell the house to us?"

"Of course. That's why I'm here."

"Oh, well, unfortunately we don't actually buy property. We make mortgage loans."

"You lend, but you don't buy?"

The worker smiled as though he sympathized with Akiyama. "You'd think that in times like these a house would move quickly on the market, but actually it isn't all that easy to sell right now."

"A mortgage would be all right, I guess...maybe that's the best way."

At this point anything to get hold of some money would do. If he got a loan, then Michiko could remain in the house.

"How much would you be able to lend?" Akiyama said. "I think the house is valued at five hundred thousand. It's an old house, though..."

The young clerk examined the floor plan attached to the title deed.

"I see. I won't know for sure until you actually show me the place. Five hundred thousand...I don't know about that. Probably we would lend only about half that amount. The manager will give you more precise details."

"Whatever you can lend me is fine, but do you have to see the place first?"

The clerk stared suspiciously at Akiyama.

"Yes, of course," he said. "We have to see it, then we have to run a check on the property at the hall of records. And we also have to meet with your wife."

Akiyama rose a little out of his chair, but then quickly settled back.

"You have to meet with my wife?"

"The deed is registered in your wife's name. We have to obtain a consent form from her saying that she agrees to the terms of the mortgage."

"A consent form?"

"That's right, sir. It's just a small formality, that's all."

Akiyama felt things going black before his eyes. Michiko would never agree to such a thing. This was no good for him. It would have been much better if he had not been so particular about keeping up appearances and had changed the name on the title deed when he had the chance.

The clerk was staring, unblinking, at the distracted, unresponsive Akiyama.

"May I have your documents for the time being?" said the clerk. "The title deed and the power of attorney? I'll give you a receipt for them."

Akiyama wasn't really paying attention any more. If he couldn't get money right away, then all this was useless.

He stood up suddenly. The young clerk, still seated, was staring at him. He nodded, then stood up as well. Akiyama had only enough time to realize that he had to get out of there quickly before they began to think that he was trying to commit fraud or absconding with property.

"Yes, well," he said, "I'm going to have to talk this over with my wife again. That is, about the amount of the loan."

"That certainly makes sense, sir. I look forward to seeing you again. If you write to us, we'd be happy to visit you."

"Thank you. I understand."

The clear autumn sun was shining in the backstreet outside, and passersby were walking along, seemingly with no cares at all. Akiyama felt a sudden urge to cry. All these people were where they ought to be, where they belonged, moving comfortably about in accordance with their daily routines. He alone was preoccupied with troubles, having suffered the indignity of that young man making him look foolish.

Atop an incline of emotions that led down to Tomiko, he concluded that all of this was Michiko's fault. She was the one who had stubbornly refused even to try to deal with their situation rationally. No matter how acerbically he spoke to her about the situation, she would not give her consent. And she was convinced that she refused out of only the best intentions.

Things were going badly for him because of his affair with Tomiko, but he refused to take responsibility, and instead blamed everything on his marriage with Michiko. All men who place no social value on the title of husband think like Akiyama.

The money he had collected from his publisher was not enough to buy them a love nest. *What should I do?* The only thing Akiyama could think about was seeing Tomiko's face and talking the matter over with her.

As he waited for her absentmindedly at the Ginza coffeehouse they had chosen for their rendezvous, he became increasingly annoyed. Tomiko had definitely run away from her home, but he had only said that he was going on a trip for two or three days. (It never occurred to him that Michiko might have opened the file case and looked for the documents.) *In any case, Tomiko can't stand Ōno. This is all just her typical self-centeredness.* Akiyama startled himself. This was the first time he had ever thought of her as selfish.

He was convinced that he and Michiko had reasons to divorce irrespective of Tomiko. Mulling over the situation, he realized that Tomiko had merely provided him an excuse. If he could not manage to make a life with her because he lacked the money, then he could always go back home again.

He realized that this calculation had been in the depths of his heart from the moment when, out of consideration for Michiko, he'd told her as a pretext that he was going on a trip.

What should I do now? I can go home, but Tomiko can't. I'd hate to send her back to Ōno, so I'll encourage her to go to her sister in Osaka. She told me she wasn't allowed to stay there, but if she just shows up, how can her sister refuse? Once that's done I can take my time to put the house in order. Then I'll call her back to Tokyo. Following this line of reasoning, Akiyama continued to think selfishly about his own desires.

Tomiko came in looking exhausted. Her makeup was a mess, and her broad forehead was exposed. Akiyama was dismayed to see a mole at the hairline along her temple that he had not noticed before.

"How did it go?" She glanced around at the men sitting there.

"It didn't. I need Michiko's consent."

"What?" She pondered the situation for a few moments. "You mean you didn't even know that much about it?"

"It's all been so abrupt."

"You mean that I've been abrupt?" Tomiko laughed.

She had not gone to a movie to relax that afternoon. Instead she visited an old school friend who ran a seamstress shop in Shinbashi. Her friend could not take Tomiko's desire to work seriously.

"What about your home?" her friend had said. "You have a child, don't you?"

"I can work that out...you see, I'm thinking of divorcing Ōno."

She went on, in exaggerated terms, to tell about all the hardships of married life. A look of admonition came over her friend's face.

"Things just don't work that way," she said. "Really, you've always been pampered. To start with, if I don't confer with Ōno, then I can't get his consent to hire you. On top of that, dressmaking is nothing like sewing children's clothes. Do you even have a sewing machine?"

Tomiko was going to have Akiyama buy her one. She could hardly tell her friend that she had a lover, and could not mention that she had already run away from home. So in the end she couldn't really discuss things fully.

Her friend appeared to have just remembered something and called in one of the seamstresses to give instructions about some work. Tomiko took advantage of the interruption and stood up.

"I envy you" she said. "You can work on your own."

"It's hard being a woman on your own. Look at the lines on my face."

"Being a wife also puts lines on your face. I really want to just throw it all aside."

"People have a hard time breaking free once they've started something. Take me. I've never been able to find a husband."

"I envy you."

"You're too extravagant," Tomiko's friend had said.

Tomiko thought that Akiyama was no match for her friend. Having told her he could not sell the house, he was already observing the expression on her face.

"So what are we going to do?" As soon as she spoke, she regretted having asked such a banal question.

"That's what I wanted to ask you."

"Why should I have an opinion? I'm just a woman."

"Because it's a problem that affects both of us."

Tomiko said nothing, showing her anger and displeasure.

"Maybe you should go to Osaka for a while," Akiyama said. "I'll get everything worked out, then I'll come and get you."

Tomiko blushed bright red.

"I knew you'd say that," she said.

Then, suddenly, the tension in her face disappeared, only to be replaced with the look of a woman who has no place to go. Akiyama recognized that expression, having seen it flicker across Michiko's face during their arguments over the past few days.

He had not known how to respond to Michiko's expression then, and he did not know how to respond to Tomiko's now.

They did not speak for a few minutes, then Tomiko said, "I'll do as you say and go to my sister's place. But I don't want you to come for me."

"All right, then, I won't go. But I can at least write to you, can't I?"

"Don't write to me either. My sister will think it's strange."

"Then what am I supposed to do? What should I do when I get everything settled?"

"You won't be able to settle anything. Just go back to Michiko. She'll be happy."

"That's terrible. I can't let you go to Osaka feeling this way."

"You can't let me? Don't try to make a fool of me. I'm not going because you said I should go. I'm going on my own...because there's no other way."

"Just stay at our place in Shinjuku a bit longer. I'll take care of things as quickly as I can."

"You mean you want me to be your mistress? I'd never accept that. To be kept by a professor...you don't have that kind of money."

Akiyama bit his lip. He felt the strength leave his hands. The face of his publisher, who would not give him enough money, and the face of the real estate clerk appeared in his mind. Akiyama hated them. As long as Tomiko said she was going to Osaka, there was nothing he could do about it. Later, if he came up with a plan that he could carry out here, he would work something out. Feeling that this was his only practical course of action, he decided to rely entirely on that uncertain thing called time.

"You're right," he said. "I don't have that kind of money. So for the time being, please go to Osaka for me."

"It's not for you!"

"I understand that."

They decided she should leave by train that evening. They had dinner at a small Japanese restaurant near the coffee shop. Tomiko drank sake.

"Tonight's my last night in Tokyo," she said.

"It's not the last. I'll come for you soon."

"You are so annoying. You say the same thing over and over. You don't know what the future holds. Everything runs it own course."

"I'll show you I can work it out."

"Tell me after you show me...I feel drunk. Can't we go some place interesting?"

"I don't know..."

"Well, excuse me. It's useless talking to you. There must be some place around here. Coming on to me can't be the only thing you know how to do. Didn't you tell me that you once went with your publisher to some French bar?"

Akiyama had gone a few times with his colleagues to a place called *Bar Peroké*. It was the kind of bar where men, driven by secret desires or boredom, came to sit in dim lighting with women who fawned on them as a way to earn the necessities of life. It was an affront to these women to have someone like Tomiko show up there. Their hostility grew especially intense when Tomiko, bored with both Akiyama, who never drank much, and the distracted hostess, who didn't know what to do with a customer accompanied by his own woman, began giving peculiar glances to all the customers around them.

"She's disgusting," said one of the hostesses.

"What a strange woman," said a man at the bar who seemed to be one of the regulars.

A strolling band that cruised the bars in the area came in and began to play a popular song. The man at the bar came over to Tomiko, bowed in an exaggerated manner, and said, "Madame, may I take your hand?"

Tomiko danced. The man's dance was obscene. At first Tomiko appeared to be amused, and stole glances at Akiyama, who was feeling uneasy. She played up to the man as if to say to Akiyama, *Look here at me!* Then all of a sudden she shoved the man away from her.

"What the hell are you doing?" The man was furious as he wiped the sweat from his face.

"Stop it now, Maa-chan." The senior hostess stepped in to put an end to it.

"Let's get out of here." Akiyama stood up.

"No," said Tomiko. "I won't go. Why did you just sit there and watch him make a fool of me? You're a coward."

Akiyama, looking like a bronze statue, tried to maintain his dignity with a brief apology to the other man.

When they got outside he tried to mollify her, saying, "It's time for the train." Tomiko wouldn't listen.

"I'm not getting on any train."

"Not getting on?"

"You think I can go to my sister's place?"

"But earlier you said...oh, never mind. If you want, we can go to Shinjuku again tonight. You're too drunk to get on a train."

"Skip it. I don't like Shinjuku. I don't like my house. I don't like anything. Shouldn't you just hurry on home now?"

She shook her hand free from Akiyama and ran into a neon-lit bar next door. Akiyama had no choice but to go in after her, and was greeted by a wall of laughter. Amid the densely billowing cigarette smoke he could make out the shining faces of laughing men. Tomiko was already sitting on one man's lap. Akiyama had no place to sit.

The same strolling band came in, almost as if it were following them. Tomiko started dancing again. She arched her neck back. She shut her eyes, which looked like flower petals, opened them wide, then shut them again.

Disconsolate thoughts constricted her chest. *Who knew what it meant to have no place to go? I can't very well go to my sister's place.* She preached her sensible sermon, then left. *She has no idea what men are really like. That's why she thinks I ought to be able to make a life with my husband.*

She remembered the summer when she was fourteen. She had gone to stay at the house in Osaka shortly after her sister's marriage. She was taking a nap one day when she felt a strange sensation on her lower belly and woke up. Her brother-in-law was sitting next to her, eyeing her breasts. When she cried out, he immediately left her and went out onto the veranda. Her sister rushed in.

"What's the matter, Tomi?"

"Nothing. I thought a bug was crawling on me," she said, rubbing her neck.

Why had she lied then? Because she knew instinctively that her brother-in-law had done something wrong. And how did she know it was wrong? Because it felt pleasant to her.

Her sister's marriage had been arranged, but at the time she and her husband were being teased by everyone for being so friendly with each other. As it turned out, her husband was the kind of man who could do such a thing to his wife's younger sister. After that Tomiko never again believed in the so-called sanctity of marriage.

The fingertips of some man who had maneuvered around behind her were touching her inappropriately. They felt exactly the same as the fingertips of her brother-in-law when she was fourteen. *Why do men always do such things to me? I never asked anyone to do that. Is there some weakness in me that makes men think it's all right for them to do as they please?*

Even Ōno's younger brother had behaved atrociously. Once, when Ōno was off to north China on business, his younger brother was bedridden with pneumonia at housing provided for the factory, which had been evacuated during the war to rural Gifu prefecture. Tomiko had gone to look after him with the best of intentions, but his expression slowly changed. One day—just three days before he died, in fact—the younger brother unexpectedly grabbed her by the arm and pulled her toward him. *Why would even a dying man do such a thing to me?*

Brothers, relatives. Men are that kind of creature. The idiot who was doing such disgusting things to me just now is still standing there. Even the man who just asked me to go to Osaka. He's the husband of Ōno's cousin. Then there's Michiko telling me, "Because Ōno's my cousin." *How I hate them all. I hate them. Cousins. Second cousins. It'd be best if they were all dead.*

She remembered Tsutomu. *That's it. I still have some place to go. How odd that I forgot all about the place I want to go to most.*

She forgot that Tsutomu was also Michiko's cousin.

When her dance partner said, "You don't need to shake your hips so much," she seized that as an excuse to break away and run outside.

Akiyama caught up with her just as she was getting into a taxi. The door closed in his face. He heard Tomiko say, "Gotanda," to the driver.

Seeing Akiyama, the driver hesitated. Tomiko shouted, "Never mind him! Get going!" Prodded by her, the driver took off.

Akiyama immediately hailed another cab and pursued Tomiko's car for some distance. When he saw the lights of Shinbashi station, however, he had a change of heart.

Who cares. She's off to that kid again. It's totally ridiculous. If she wants to go to his place, regardless of the consequences, then let her do as she pleases. It's not my problem anymore.

A man like Akiyama can take action only after being humiliated.

He got out of the taxi. The lights of the station had reminded him of home, and so he decided to go back to Hake.

Tsutomu was in his apartment. Tomiko did not look at his face.

"I'm here now," she said. "If it's all right with you." Like a bird looking for an escape, she bumped up against the walls on three sides of the narrow room, then collapsed on top of Tsutomu.

The large eyes, the pleasure-seeking heart that lived in this drunken body, which no longer seemed human, created an impression of voluptuousness for him.

That night, for the first time, Tsutomu slept with a married woman. He noticed that there was no difference at all between the body of a wife and the bodies of the women students he was familiar with.

Akiyama sniffed an odor drifting from his house. It was sandalwood incense, a scent familiar to him because Michiko's father had been fond of it. *This again?* The sensation he'd had all through his marriage to Michiko of being oppressed by the Miyaji family stirred back to life again. He now regretted that he had been unable to work out some way to live with Tomiko.

When he went into his bedroom, he was greeted by a strange spectacle. Michiko was lying on the bedding in her kimono. The incense in the burner near the pillow had gone out, and the nightstand had fallen over.

Michiko seemed to be in a deep sleep. She had applied a light coat of make-up to her face, which was as motionless as a stone. Traces of dried tears streaked her makeup from the corners of her eyes to her ears.

He called her name and shook her, but she did not move. Seeing her knees bound together by *obi* cords, Akiyama knew this wasn't normal. He pulled her eyelids open and saw that the pupils were constricted like the eye of a cat. They were not moving.

Akiyama let out a cry, and his jaw dropped.

He saw a glass on the desk. A whitish substance had settled to the bottom. He was reluctant to stick his fingertip in and taste it.

Standing in the middle of the room, looking at the sleeping face of Michiko, who was dressed in a kimono, he was seized with despair. *This is just like her. She always goes through life putting on her finest.*

In a panic, he tried to think what he should do. It was just past eleven o'clock. He judged from the fact that all the doors had been closed that Michiko probably took the medicine in the evening. Maybe only two or three hours had passed. If she got medical help soon, she'd be all right.

There was no one else in the house. If possible, he wanted to take care of things on his own. However, he had to tell Ōno at some point, so the best thing was to get Ōno's help right away.

Ōno was still up. He had finally received a telegram from the sister in Osaka: *Tomi not here.* He had been thinking about where he should go tomorrow to search for Tomiko. When he saw Akiyama rush in with a stricken look on his face, he assumed that something terrible had happened to his wife. Upon hearing about Michiko, he became even more flustered. Luckily, the old woman who helped him happened to be there and agreed to stay on that night. He asked her to watch Yukiko and rushed off through the darkened streets to the Miyaji house.

"I was too careless," Ōno said in a voice that sounded as if he had at last come to his senses.

"Did Michiko say something?"

Ōno's eyes flashed in the dark. "You of all people should have thought about that. Tomiko has been gone since yesterday."

Akiyama was silent. Ōno left him in front of the house and hurried on to call the family doctor. He noticed from the outset that Akiyama had expressed no surprise that Tomiko was not at home. *That's right, isn't it. I'm going to have to check into that later.* Once he returned with the doctor, however, he had no opportunity to question Akiyama.

The doctor was calm. He examined Michiko and said, "This sort of thing is common. It's probably too late to make her vomit, but I think she should be fine."

Ōno suggested that they cut her brocade *obi* off. Akiyama turned her body carefully and loosened it. The doctor tilted her head back and used a penlight to examine her pupils.

"This is serious," he said. "It looks as though she's given up on life. But remember, if the worst happens, it isn't the husband's fault. No one can stop a person from taking an overdose of medicine of their own free will." This was a strange kind of reassurance for a doctor to be giving.

Injecting Ringer's solution into her thigh to protect against dehydration, he also gave her an injection to stimulate her heart. "This is normal procedure," he said. "In four or five hours she may be in a delirium. But that's normal, too. I'll drop by in the morning." The doctor went home, and after Ōno massaged in the traces of the Ringer's solution, he spoke to Akiyama.

"I'm going home now. You look after her. You're going to pay for this later. You are."

A long time passed and Akiyama heard a sound. Was it a groan? A laugh? It rose from deep in Michiko's throat. To Akiyama that sound, which had to have a physical source, was like the voice of Michiko's heart. If wailing ghosts really exist, he thought they must sound like this.

The voice stopped abruptly, and the room was once more filled with the still-ness of the night. Occasionally the spasmodic movements of Michiko's hands striking the sheets mingled with the stillness.

As dawn neared a human voice broke from Michiko's mouth. It was a crying voice. "Tomu-chan," she called out, "Tomu-chan!" It was Tsutomu's childhood nick-name. According to the doctor, this crying out was the first sign of her revival.

Akiyama checked her pulse. It was weak. Her pupils were still constricted. Tears were flowing from her sightless eyes.

"Tomu-chan. I've left it to you. I'm poor now, but I'll give you what I have. Please don't be so reckless."

What was all this about? Akiyama, noticing the documents he had tossed aside, quickly put them back into the file case.

"Tomu-chan. You look silly in those old army clothes. So haughty and proud of yourself. Don't be silly. Going off to war doesn't mean you're distinguished. Stop being so haughty...wearing such clothes."

A contented look appeared on her face, lingering a few moments. Then she started to cry again.

"I'm no good. I have to die. If I don't, you'll never be happy. What? What is it? Die together? Don't be foolish. Do you really know where I'm going? It's bitter, this medicine. Even when I mix it with water, it's bitter. It sinks right to the bottom. Did you know I had to drink such bitter stuff?"

She tilted her throat back as though she were drinking something. Her move-ments aroused a visceral response in Akiyama. He found it hard to breathe. This was all for Tsutomu. He told himself, *It's none of my business.*

"No, that won't do. You have to live. Life is precious. But...to do such a thing...with a woman like Tomiko . It's wrong. Don't do it. With another man's wife...

142

if you're going to, do it with me. I'm no good, so it doesn't matter what happens to my body. Do it with me. No, not that. Be gentle. No, that sort of...it doesn't matter. It doesn't matter what happens to my body. I'm going to die. So...no, don't do it with Tomiko."

Tears continued to pour from her blinded eyes, soaking her hair. Reason and will had left Michiko, and only her heart remained alive. A heart filled with love and jealousy being torn asunder by despair.

"Tomu-chan! Tomu-chan!" She called his name repeatedly in a loud voice, stretching out her arms.

Dawn finally broke, and Akiyama could hear the sounds of early risers in the neighborhood. Akiyama was worried that they might hear Michiko crying out, so he allowed her arms, which were groping the air, to embrace him.

"It's Tsutomu," he said.

"Tomu-chan? Is it really you? When did you get here? Why didn't you come earlier? I made sure the back door was unlocked. Will you die with me? You know that's not right. You have to live. It's bitter. To have to drink such foul, bitter stuff. What? You say you're a soldier? You're not afraid? You're foolish. Is it so great to have gone to war?"

She kept repeating her words. She tilted her throat back again and again as if she were drinking something. Akiyama was now experiencing the pain of a husband whose wife does not call out his name on her deathbed. Clenching his teeth, he jumped away from the bed. Michiko started crying out again, so he put a folded cushion into her arms. Michiko clutched it, and continued to murmur caressing words of love.

The doctor arrived with a nurse. Hearing Michiko's delirium, he smiled. "So it's started," he said. But when he took her pulse he cocked his head in puzzlement.

"Has your wife had any problems with her heart?"

"I don't know. She told me once that her heart was weak when she was little."

"I have to tell you that there's some cause for concern, though I'm not sure how serious this is." The doctor ordered the nurse, in a slightly sharp manner, to prepare "two doses." He gave Michiko an injection of a strong stimulant.

"Is Mr. Ōno coming here?" the doctor said.

"Yes, he should be here soon."

"I'll have the nurse stay with you. Please try not to worry too much," he said, and hurried back to his home.

Akiyama was now prepared for the worst. He realized that if Michiko died his reputation would be ruined—that he would be labeled by society as a man who caused his wife's suicide because he had pursued his own pleasure. He hated Michiko. Then he thought, *No matter what people say, she died for Tsutomu. I never imagined those*

143

photographs could lead to this. That was wrong. But whatever the cause, she did not die for me.

Presently, Michiko seemed to realize that she was still alive, that her suicide attempt had failed.

"Tomu-chan. Please bring the medicine to me. There's some left over there. If I drink it, everything will be fine. Tomu-chan. You're the only one I can rely on. Bring it here quickly. Why don't you listen to me?"

Ōno arrived with Yukiko. Michiko cried out in their presence, calling out Tsutomu's name in her loudest voice. Slowly her voice weakened. Then she began to clutch at her chest with both hands, as though she were trying to pull the collars of her robe together.

"It hurts so, I can't take anymore. It's too much. Too much."

It was purely an accident that Michiko's suicide attempt did not fail. If her death had not been an accident, then no tragedy could be said to have taken place. That's the way tragedy is in the twentieth century.

Ōno was crying. He turned to Michiko, whose breathing was becoming imperceptible, and called to her, "You're terrible...you're selfish to kill yourself. It's not just you. Don't you know that by killing yourself you're killing those who love you?"

At the end she said, "Help me." Hearing the normal tone of those abnormal words, Akiyama shuddered.

Even at that moment, however, he firmly believed that Michiko had died for Tsutomu's sake. He would not accept that she had died because he left her.

This professor, caught up in the literature that was the subject of his lectures, was always outside of humanity.

Because of the way he had treated his own wife, Ōno was also outside of humanity; but his behavior toward her after she ran away brought him back in. Akiyama was staring at the still face of his wife, who had stopped breathing. He was crying from emotions he never knew he possessed. He let slip the words, "I'm sorry," and told Ōno where Tomiko was. As soon as he heard this, Ōno left with Yukiko, who had been wandering about the house upset.

He showed up smiling in front of Tsutomu and Tomiko. They had dressed early in the morning and were sitting together in mutual silence.

"I see you helped Tomiko out last night. I'm sorry for all the trouble. Thank you," said Ōno.

Yukiko was cowering behind Ōno. Tomiko smiled and pulled her close. Tomiko had always known there was no future for her and Tsutomu.

Tsutomu said nothing throughout all this. As Ōno escorted Tomiko out, Tsutomu was staring at his broad back, which he saw as a symbol of society. Even so, he felt he should not have committed adultery just to break society down.

He knew how to break things, and he thought it was all right to gamble his own life, having died once in Burma. He lost hope only when he considered what would become of his vow to Michiko.

Just as he was stepping out of the apartment, Ōno realized that he had not told Tsutomu that Michiko was dead. He hastily pulled Tomiko back inside.

The human heart is a strange thing. Ōno tried to put on a brave front, but his heart was already strained by this setting, where he had quietly taken back his faithless wife. He lacked the imagination to be able to recognize the nature of the love between Tsutomu and Michiko, but he was able to sense, at that moment, that the news of Michiko's death had transformed Tsutomu into a kind of monster. And he was afraid.

Translator's Postscript

At noon on August 15, 1945 the Japanese government broadcast a recording of Hirohito, the Emperor of Japan, reading the rescript that announced his nation's surrender. Hirohito's words were extraordinary in many ways, not least because they truly may be said to have marked the exact moment when one historical period ended and another began.

For most Japanese in 1945, the age just ended had ultimately proved tragic, but it was a period that could be read in hindsight as a coherent, if simplistic, narrative. Beginning in the mid-nineteenth century with the forced abandonment of Japan's policy of self-imposed isolation, the nation emerged at the turn of the twentieth century as a global military and colonial power whose dream of empire in Asia was ultimately destroyed by the reckless pursuit of war and conquest.

Applying similar powers of hindsight, many Japanese today would read the age begun on August 15, 1945 as an equally coherent, if still open-ended, narrative. The hardships of occupation life and reform paved the way for the achievement of a conservative political consensus and of economic growth that resulted in the reemergence of Japan as a superpower. Of course it goes without saying that this comforting retrospective of the postwar was inconceivable to the Japanese in 1945. For them the new age that began with Hirohito's rescript had neither narrative form nor historical meaning, but loomed as a void that presented at best an uncertain, chaotic prospect.

As memories of the experience of the immediate postwar period fade, the sheer scale of the uncertainty and chaos slowly become harder to recover on a personal, individual level. Yet even now, a bare outline of the historical record can call up powerful images of the bleakness of the situation Japan faced in 1945. At least three million Japanese had died in the war, with millions more sick, wounded, or malnourished. The material culture and the economic infrastructure of large sections of the country, especially the industrialized zones of urban areas, had been nearly wiped out. Basic governmental services and the flow of goods were seriously disrupted.

Accompanying the physical destruction wrought by the war was a shattering of spirit, a kind of psychic destruction that led to widespread malaise and demoralization. Guilt over the murderous conduct of the Japanese military throughout Asia and the Pacific was compounded by the grievances that came from a sense of victimization. The devastating emotions fueled by guilt and the humiliation of defeat were made even more bitter by the awareness that Japan's losses had been in vain. Veterans were often treated with disdain, and some victims at home—war widows, orphans, and even survivors of the atomic bombings—faced indifference and discrimination. Through all of this, many Japanese never had the opportunity to properly mourn, either because loved ones did not return, or because the sheer effort to survive took priority.

The spiritual wreckage was symbolized by the flourishing of the black market and the sex trade. The black market was for a time the only viable outlet for many goods, yet its cutthroat practices and scofflaw attitude heightened awareness of social disorder. The brash and public nature of prostitution, much of the trade geared specifically to serve the American conquerors, was a constant reminder of the hardships facing women and of Japan's subservience and fall from the status of colonizer to that of colonized. The turn of many younger people to a life of decadent self-gratification in the face of all this turmoil was perhaps an expression of release after nearly two decades of repression and self-sacrifice. The pursuit of decadence may even have been an explicit slap at the delusions and hypocrisy of wartime leadership. Whatever motives lay behind the celebration of self-indulgence, however, the phenomenon was seen as yet another sign of the breakdown of order and values.

The realities and the perceptions of social upheaval were reinforced by the legal and economic reforms imposed by the occupation authorities. These changes fundamentally challenged not just the accepted norms of the prewar period, but also many of the basic institutions that reflected and sustained those norms. The system of primogeniture that determined inheritance and the laws governing property rights were amended; the legal status of women was altered with the constitutional conferral of a range of political, legal, and human rights; the military and the governmental structures that supported it were abolished; rights to assemble, to organize trade unions and political organizations, and to exercise free speech were extended; the practices and structures of many of the largest business firms were brought under regulatory control. The effect of these changes went well beyond the primary aims of the occupation to demilitarize and democratize Japan, transforming the ways in which Japanese understood basic categories of self and identity, of gender, family, and nation.

Given this range of crises and transformations, it is reasonable to expect that Japan might have experienced a period of stunned silence, or of cultural paralysis after the war. But the preceding outline of the turmoil after 1945 is not the whole, or even the most important aspect, of the history of the period. What is in fact most remarkable is that despite all the chaos—or perhaps *because* of the chaos—the late 1940s began a period of extraordinary creativity in many fields. Indeed, it is no exaggeration to claim that the two decades following the war were among the most productive periods, both culturally and economically, in recent Japanese history.

It is tempting to attribute the postwar burst of creativity to sheer necessity, but in fact there is no single explanation for what happened. One important contributing factor may be that, even in the face of the censorship enforced by the occupation authorities, many people actually felt a sense of liberation and possibility. The occupation reforms may have been disruptive of values and social institutions, their aims may have even been contradictory at times, but their impact on the economy and on the legal and political status of individuals contributed in real ways to a feeling of newfound freedom. That sense of liberation was manifested in many ways, but achievements in the literary arts may be taken as representative of this particular phenomenon of postwar culture.

A number of writers whose reputations were secure before the war, such as Tanizaki Jun'ichirō or Kawabata Yasunari, entered new and productive phases of their careers. Some prominent prewar figures, such as Kikuchi Kan, saw their reputations diminished or ruined because of their support of the military government, but such purges opened up opportunities for a new generation of writers. Many leftists, who had been suppressed or who had been forced to make public conversions in support of the emperorism of the 1930s, reemerged and energized the literary scene with their ideas and with their often painfully self-reflective debates on the price of collaboration. A group referred to as the first generation, which included among others Sakaguchi Ango, Noma Hiroshi, Shiina Rinzō, and Dazai Osamu, rose to prominence, bringing fresh and iconoclastic perspectives that captured the temper of the times. Within a little more than a decade of the defeat, an astonishing array of talent—Mishima Yukio, Abe Kōbō, Enchi Fumiko, Ōe Kenzaburō, Koda Aya, Endō Shūsaku—was producing memorable works of art.

Although this catalogue of tragedy and coping, of turmoil and achievement, is too brief and sweeping to adequately convey the complexity of the period, my aim in presenting it is to provide at least a broad sense of the historical and artistic contexts in which A Wife in Musashino was composed. Of all the literary talents who emerged in the late 1940s, a compelling case can be made that Ōoka Shōhei (1909–88) best represented in his work the ethical and spiritual crises confronting his age. Whether writing about the experience of battle, or about the profound effects of defeat, Ōoka found a voice that is truly distinctive, that was recognized and honored in its day, and that continues to speak even now with power and clarity.

Before examining how A Wife in Musashino exemplifies Ōoka's achievement as an artist, we need to consider briefly another crucial element of the historical context of its composition, which is the personal background of the author. Born and raised in Tokyo, Ōoka's mother was a former geisha and his father was a stockbroker who made his fortune speculating in the market. Ōoka had a comfortable early life, and in 1921 entered the middle school of Aoyama Gakuin, a Christian mission academy. For a time he showed interest in Christian teachings, but the long-lasting impact of his early education was the opportunity it gave him to read widely in Western literature. In 1927 he began to study the French language, and two years later he enrolled in the prestigious Department of French at Kyoto Imperial University. While at Kyoto he made a number of literary friends and wrote for student publications. When he graduated in 1932 he chose to pursue a literary career with the support of the influential critic, Kobayashi Hideo. Ōoka tried his hand at fiction, but most of his output during the 1930s consisted of critical studies and translations, which he found outlets for in journals such as *Sakuhin* and *Bungakkai*.

In 1933 he read *The Charterhouse of Parma* by Stendhal (Marie-Henri Beyle), a novel that made a lasting impression. From that point on he immersed himself in the study of Stendhal's works, and over the next decade published several critical volumes and translations. Of course, Ōoka had a number of other literary interests, including the works of André Gide, Raymond Radiguet, and the great Japanese novelist Natsume Sōseki. But of all the early influences on him, several characteristics shared by Stendhal and Sōseki proved to be especially attractive to Ōoka: their irony and skeptical distance, their sensitivity to class distinctions, and their anxiety about the place of the individual in modern society. As a member of an important literary coterie centered on Kobayashi, Ōoka read the fiction of Stendhal and Sōseki within an intellectual climate that saw nothing but unbridled egoism in the consciousness of Western modernity. His early career thus coincided with a period when many of his contemporaries were obsessed with finding a way out of the trap of individualism, and filled with an unrequited desire to return to an essential culture authentic to Japan. The critical frame of mind he cultivated during this time would prove crucial to the later development of his own art.

Although Ōoka was productive throughout the 1930s, he was not able to support himself by his writing. In 1938 he took a job as a translator for the Imperial Oxygen Co., Ltd., a French-Japanese joint venture. Late in 1943 he moved to Kawasaki Heavy Industries, where he worked for a few months in the Materials Division of the Kobe Shipyard. Soon after, in early 1944, he was drafted into the Army, and in July he was sent to Mindoro Island in the Philippines. Following the American invasion on December 15th, he was taken prisoner in January 1945. Ill from malaria and traumatized by combat, Ōoka spent several months in a POW camp. He was repatriated in December 1945.

These experiences provided him with one of the central subjects of his career, which he treated in works of fiction, history, and autobiography. In the horrors of the battlefield he found a voice unique in its authoritative tone. Ōoka was an intellectually mature and technically polished craftsman when he left for the Philippines;

but the violence of war sharpened an already skeptical sensibility—a temperament that longed for genuine values even as it accepted the impossibility of ever satisfying that desire. Starting at points of contact where individual lives intersect with the forces of history, Ōoka returns again and again in his work to an exploration of the tension between the need for self-realization and the need for something beyond the self. The extreme nature of the experience of war and defeat reduces life to such basic instincts of human nature that it makes the determination of right action difficult. The only apparent solution in such a circumstance is an appeal to personal autonomy and freedom as the ultimate ground of authentic values and meaning.

The emphasis Ōoka gives in his writings generally to problems of human perspective, knowledge, and judgment has led some critics to read him as a cynic.[1] No doubt a high degree of skepticism about the sincerity of human intentions and motives and about the possibility of achieving moral certainty is a recurring element in most of Ōoka's work. To call him a cynic, however, misleadingly implies that Ōoka is not searching for the ground of right action, but already assumes it does not exist. A number of critics in Japan, including Nakano Kōji and Isoda Kōichi, have suggested that it might be more accurate to see in Ōoka's literary method a kind of stoicism—albeit a stoicism bordering on the cynical. Isoda in particular argues that there is a hidden longing for purity, or immaculateness, beyond Ōoka's reputed cynicism.[2]

Isoda points to a key feature of Ōoka's writings, which is the gap between the subjectivity of desires and intents and the purity and universal detachment of ideals. Ōe Kenzaburō, writing in 1966, described this feature in similar terms, noting that Ōoka's works possess a universality achieved by an understanding and aesthetic intuition that "transcends the so-called postwar" and a subjectivity "permeated by the postwar."[3] The ambivalence with which many Japanese have confronted their wartime past and the historical contours and meanings of Ōoka's writings are located, as Ōe observed, at the center of the larger cultural conflict that is Japan's struggle with modernity.

The ethical and aesthetic power of Ōoka's work derives from his acute sense of a breach between universal ideals of morality and the aspirations of individuals. There is a sense that human desires are inescapable, but that apparent cynicism is tempered by his artistic quest for a subtler language that can express something meaningful beyond the self. The longing for purity that Isoda locates at the heart of Ōoka's literary method is a fusion of aesthetic form and ethical ideal that creates a skeptical

---

[1]This is a widely held critical assessment of Ōoka. For examples of this kind of response in Japan see Kojima Nobuo's article "Ōoka Shōhei to shinishizumu," in Nihon bungaku kenkyū shiryō kankōkai, ed., *Ōoka Shōhei, Fukunaga Takehiko* (Tokyo: Yūseidō, 1978), pp. 50-56.

[2] See Nakano Kōji, *Zettai reido no bungaku* [The literature of absolute zero] (Tokyo: Shūeisha, 1976), pp. 100-117. For Isoda's remarks see *Ōoka Shōhei, Fukunaga Takehiko*, p. 80.

[3] Cited in Ikeda Jun'ichi, *Ōoka Shōhei* (Tokyo: Tōjūsha, 1979), p. 41.

narrative mode, a critical consciousness that strives to achieve a total integration of the subjective motivations and actions of individual characters with external historical and social realities.

A *Wife in Musashino* is a brilliantly realized example of Ōoka's method. The novel was originally published serially in the literary journal *Gunzō* from January to September 1950. The timing of its publication is significant in that it was composed simultaneously with portions of Ōoka's great war novel, *Fires on the Plain*. Ōoka had begun serializing *Fires on the Plain* in the journal *Buntai* from December 1948 to July 1949, but when *Buntai* folded before he could finish the novel, he decided to rewrite even as he began preparing *A Wife in Musashino* for publication. The conception of the revised version of *Fires on the Plain*, which finally appeared in the magazine *Tenbō* from January to August 1951, thus shares a number of thematic and stylistic elements with *A Wife in Musashino*. Although the two novels stand alone as works of literary art, they are nonetheless linked to each other, as obverse and reverse, by their depiction of the effects of war and defeat overseas and at home.

The reception of *A Wife in Musashino* helped to cement Ōoka's reputation, which had been established by the publication of his memoir *Furyoki* (POW diary, translated as *Taken Captive*). The novel was a critical and commercial success, and the writer and critic Fukuda Tsuneari[4] quickly adapted it for a film version, which was directed by Mizoguchi Kenji and released in 1951.[5] I believe the reasons for the appeal of the story are apparent, but to understand the aesthetic sources of that appeal requires that we read the novel with an eye to Japan's postwar conditions.

Ōoka's propensity to strive for the perfection of a subtler language that is precise, rational, and accurate was stimulated by his early engagement with Stendhal. Erich Auerbach has observed that the aspect of Stendhal's fiction that made it a significant literary phenomenon was its ability to logically and systematically situate the imagined lives of his characters "within the most concrete kind of contemporary history."[6] The effect of this characteristic of Stendhal's fiction on Ōoka's literary practice

---

[4] Fukuda was one of the most influential commentators on Ōoka's literary art. He was one of the first critics to describe Ōoka's sensibility as a kind of stoicism, and he made very strong claims for the importance of *A Wife in Musashino*, which he saw as a ground-breaking work as important to postwar literature as Futabatei Shimei's novel, *Ukigumo* (Drifting Clouds), was to literature of the Meiji period. See his *Sakkaron* (Essays on authors) in *Fukuda Tsuneari hyōronshū* (Collected criticism of Fukuda Tsuneari), v. 3 (Tokyo: Shinchōsha, 1966), pp. 303–37.

[5] The English title of this release is *The Lady of Musashino*. One way to translate *fujin* is "lady," and, in the sense of someone who is accomplished in manners and conduct, "lady" is an appropriate choice. However, the word "lady" also carries the connotation of aristocratic status, and that is a problem in this case. To avoid any possible confusion with regard to social status, I have chosen to translate the title as *A Wife in Musashino*. My choice stresses Michiko's status as a wife and, more important, suggests the value she herself places on her status.

[6] Erich Auerbach, *Mimesis: The Representation of Reality in Western Literature*, tr. Willard R. Trask (Princeton: Princeton University Press, 1968), pp. 457–58.

was decisive, but it was also tempered in a crucial way by Ōoka's personal experience of war. The day-to-day struggle for survival surely heightened his skeptical outlook toward any actions and motives not grounded in material reality, but they also nurtured an empathetic understanding of the nature of suffering. Ōoka's critical consciousness enabled him to write with logical precision and, at times, acerbity without his voice becoming cold, abstract, or attenuated. This quality permeates every narrative element of A Wife in Musashino.

Ōoka so fully situates the motives and attitudes of his characters within contemporary history that his novel almost incidentally provides a snapshot of the state of Japan in 1947, when most of the action takes place. The subcultures of the black market, of the panpan (the prostitutes who show up in bars and in the areas around Koganei station and Tsutomu's apartment in Gotanda), and of decadent college students all provide an unobtrusive, but fully realized, backdrop to the story. This kind of closely observed detail contributes not merely to the formal realism of the novel, but also to an atmosphere of license and desperation that sets off the tragedy of Michiko and Tsutomu.

Ōoka pays close attention as well to the physical, spatial settings in which human relationships are situated. Many of these spaces provide visual evidence of the ongoing presence of war and defeat in 1947: the burnt-out ruins around Ebara; the deforested fields near Hake; the abandoned factory and airfield that Tsutomu explores; the untended park near Gotanda; the shabby hotels at Sayama ruined by the wartime economy. These spaces give a vivid sense of contemporary history not only by their specificity, but also by their relationship to the most important space in the novel, the topography of the Musashino plateau. Local spaces in the novel are explicitly linked to recent history, but they are grounded in a landscape that possesses both deep-rooted cultural and mythic associations, and a material reality that is indifferent to the transience of human history.

Musashino is a city in the east-central area of the Tokyo metropolis that occupies what was once an agricultural region (traces of its agrarian past are noted throughout the novel). Following the Great Kantō Earthquake of 1923, this rural district was developed as a residential suburb, and the central shopping districts of Kichijōji and Inokashira Park have been popular for several decades. The city name, Musashino, is derived from its location in the Musashino plateau, a diluvial upland in the southwestern Kantō plain that extends from present-day Tokyo to Saitama prefecture. The name means "the plains of Musashi," Musashi being one of the fifteen provinces of the Tōkaidō region of central Japan established by the Taika Reforms of 646. This province encompassed much of what is now Tokyo, as well as Saitama and eastern sections of Kanagawa prefectures. The province was administered directly at various times by a succession of important military clans—the Minamoto, the Uesugi, the Tokugawa—and so the name Musashi conjures up images of Japan's martial history. The ability of the name to call forth these cultural associations in recent times is apparent in the decision of the Imperial Navy to name its two largest battleships of the Second World War Musashi and Yamato.[7]

Ōoka situates his story within a landscape that simultaneously represents contemporary history and mythic memory. The settings provide more than mere background detail, however. The depiction of the main characters—their personalities, habits of mind, and even their physical appearance—draws heavily on the deeply rooted cultural associations evoked by place. Eudora Welty has famously noted the importance of place to the literary arts, and has argued that skillful evocation of place through words has everything to do with making characters real:

> Place in fiction is the named, identified, concrete, exact and exacting, and therefore credible, gathering spot of all that has been felt, is about to be experienced, in the novel's progress. Location pertains to feeling; feeling profoundly pertains to place; place in history partakes of feeling, as feeling about history partakes of place.[8]

Welty offers her comments not as a romanticized glorification of space, but as a practical consideration of an element in the rhetorical art of fiction writing. As such, her views help to shed light on Ōoka's practice of that art in A Wife in Musashino.

Ōoka evokes multiple planes of space to give specificity and depth to his characters, and to enable the reader to imagine their consciousness and motivations. The adulterous lovers, Akiyama and Tomiko, are shallow, selfish, and morally reprehensible, but they are not incomprehensible. Both of them are out of place in the worlds they inhabit; it is psychological and cultural displacement that brings them together, even though they are not in love. Akiyama is a descendant of peasants who marries Michiko, a descendant of a hatamoto family (samurai who once served the shogun) as a way to climb the social ladder. His life story is a particular version of a more general type of narrative told frequently in modern Japan—that is, the story of a young man coming from the provinces and making his way in Tokyo. This kind of worldly success story became a defining cultural myth, told countless times in fiction, plays, and films. The geographical poles of traditional village and modern metropolis consistently define the narrative parameters of this myth and create an inherently dramatic tension. Success in the modern world of Tokyo is desired, but even when it is achieved it always comes at the cost of spiritual displacement and loss of identity.

Following the pattern of this modern myth, Akiyama's success is double-edged. He overcomes the disadvantages of his birthplace and escapes his family past,

---

[7] Yamato is sometimes used as an alternative name for Japan, but in ancient times it was the name of a province, now Nara prefecture, closely associated with the culture of the imperial family.
[8] Eudora Welty, "Place in Fiction," in On Writing (New York: Modern Library, 2002), pp. 46-47.

but his newfound status as an intellectual and literati is not enough to satisfy the desire and ambition that drove him to seek a new life in Tokyo. One of the primary reasons for his dissatisfaction is that the very emblem of his success, his marriage to Michiko, serves as a constant reminder of his former status, his place in society. Akiyama is not of Hake, and he does everything to avoid that place until the American bombing campaign during the final stages of the war leaves him no option. Once he has moved to Michiko's family home at Hake, Akiyama's resentment grows until it reaches the point where he is driven to take revenge.

Akiyama's resentments are not entirely without justification. He bears on his body, in his personal appearance, the marks of his native place. Slight and dark-skinned, he is self-conscious of his peasant heritage, not least because of the caste discrimination he suffers at the hands of Michiko's brothers and her father, Miyaji. The evocation of place in the literary portrait of Akiyama deepens our understanding of his motives, which, though not entirely beyond our sympathies, are ultimately frightening in their capacity for vindictiveness. Akiyama is sly, self-serving, opportunistic, and cowardly, and his interest in the fiction of Stendhal is derived from his identification with characters like Julien Sorel, an ambitious social climber read by Akiyama as a sophisticated romantic hero. Akiyama's misreading of Stendhal is a knowing gesture of self-deprecation on Ōoka's part, but it is a detail that is at once satiric and poignant. For Akiyama is spiritually homeless; his displacement is an analogue to his lack of moral consciousness, to the complex, confused mix of yearning and ambition that defines his character and helps propel the plot to its tragic end.

Tomiko is also not of Hake. She is an outsider trapped in a loveless, cynical, and abusive marriage. If Akiyama typifies the myth of the young man on the rise, Tomiko typifies another cultural type, the *moga*, or modern girl—a stereotyped figure that arose in the 1920s whose Westernized beauty, vivaciousness, and sexual license suggested the simultaneous lure and danger of modern culture. Tomiko's milieu is the modern city; and, befitting her background, she is perhaps the most rootless of all the characters in the novel. Because her father was a corporate executive, she had to move with her family from place to place during her childhood. She picked up customs and manners from Tokyo, Osaka, and Nagoya, but she was never grounded anywhere. The fact that she can affect the behavior of many places is not, in her case, the mark of a cosmopolitan, but that of a woman who is essentially formless and empty.

The qualities that define Tomiko make her seem less developed than the other characters for much of the novel. Ōoka's design is to describe and treat her initially as a stereotype—the coquette, the flirt. Tomiko is all fashion and show, all body and appetite; and like Akiyama, she is resentful of, and dissatisfied with, her place in society. Because she is so rootless and restless, she is also capricious and headstrong; and those traits create the impression that Tomiko's motivations are less specific than those of the other characters. By the end of the novel, however, the effectiveness of Ōoka's design becomes clear as Tomiko develops into a fully realized character. Nurtured in the culture of the modern metropolis, her identity is tied not to inner qualities, but to outer surface. Her consciousness is drawn not from a spiritual core, but from the gaze of others, especially men. Tomiko tries to satisfy her longings and desires through the only power—the only capital—she has, which is her body. She is empowered and victimized by her looks, though she lacks the moral consciousness to understand completely why she is trapped. Nonetheless, her motivations, the causes of her resentment, are not fully revealed to us until near the end of the novel when we learn that her brother-in-law made sexual advances to her when she was just fourteen. This revelation by itself does not explain everything, but the act of self-reflection that calls forth the memory of her childhood trauma gives a depth, an interior reality, to Tomiko that helps us understand the full force of her destructiveness. It is important to note that this moment of memory and self-reflection occurs at a hostess bar, the kind of place where male eyes and hands caress women and turn them into objects. Ōoka's artistry is apparent in the skill with which he depicts the space of the demimonde of the Tokyo bar scene in order to endow Tomiko with her conflicted identity as a manipulative coquette and as a victim who is always a sexual object.

Ōoka's ability to use place to depict the subtle nuances of social and class distinctions in order to lay bear the resentments and prejudices of his characters is one that he shares with Natsume Sōseki; and we see that skill brought to bear in the creation of the character of Tomiko's husband, Ōno. Ōno is not a central character, but his presence in the story adds an important dimension to the atmosphere of moral decay. He is a hustler whose shady and reckless business dealings call to mind all the excesses of wartime profiteering and the black market. His concern with keeping up the appearance of high social status, and his desire to possess the more showy aspects of modern culture are apparent in his choice of wife and in the style of his home. Driven and superficial, he is every bit as egotistical and selfish as Akiyama and Tomiko. However, he is also connected to Hake in a way that they are not, and that connection gives his character a grounding that Akiyama in particular lacks.

Although Ōno turns his back on the more traditional aspects of Hake to pursue his delusional fancies, his identity is more firmly fixed because he can claim descent from samurai stock. His class-consciousness is the source of his prejudices, his perverse mischievousness, his lack of self-awareness, his pretentiousness, and his buffoonery. Yet for all that, he has some nascent sense of himself and of his responsibilities as a husband and father—a sense that Akiyama recognizes and scorns—and he has at least a basic, if unsophisticated, core of moral awareness that enables him to forgive his wife and to recognize the horror of Tsutomu's final transformation. Ōno is a vivid literary creation because Ōoka has identified him with his place, with the concrete and exact items of home and garden that reflect his tastes, his status, and his human weaknesses.

Michiko, the central figure of the novel, is the only one who feels at home in Hake, who is firmly rooted in and identified with a single place. She is accustomed to the area around Musashino—its flora and fauna, its topography—even though she has never formally studied it. The identification of character with place is one of the main ways that Ōoka connects Michiko with traditional culture and values. Her upbringing and family history, as the last direct descendant of the Miyaji family, is another important marker of her connection to traditional values. The cultural associations of Hake and Musashino and the personal history of her family combine to make Michiko what she is: a wife. Unlike all the other characters, she has a highly developed moral consciousness and a stable center of identity. Because she has so fully internalized her role as wife, her sense of self is unassailable; and because she has so fully internalized the virtues that come with her role, she has no more need to reason out what is right or good than she has to study the topography of Musashino. She knows what is right and good, and so she is not driven by the desires, resentments, longing, or delusion that destabilize the lives of Akiyama, Tomiko, and Ōno.

Michiko's stability, her rootedness, is the source of her strength and identity; but in the end that very quality is the cause of her tragedy. Although she is not displaced and adrift at the beginning of her married life with Akiyama, she is nevertheless a figure out of her time. For better or worse, as the age passes her by, the values that give meaning and significance to her identity also pass. This is a point that Ōoka draws explicitly to the reader's attention by the epigraph that identifies Michiko with Radiguet's heroine, the Countess d'Orgel. Ōoka makes the same point even more strongly in a short essay he wrote after the novel appeared that set forth his intentions. He claimed that he appended the epigraph in order to be fair to the reader and indicate his debt to the methods of Radiguet. More important, he insisted that one of his aims was to defend the old-fashioned modesty (*kofū na teishuku*) of his heroine, Michiko.[9] The word *teishuku* conveys more than just modesty. It refers to a range of wifely virtues, including devotion and chastity. Ōoka's phrase "old-fashioned modesty" neatly captures the two key aspects of Michiko's life: her role and status as traditional wife, and the anachronism of that role in 1947. Thus, although the novel is generally sympathetic to Michiko, it highlights both the inflexibility of her character and the precariousness of her situation.

Michiko's tragedy unfolds when she is confronted with two crises. The first arises when she falls in love with her cousin, Tsutomu. Some critics in Japan have described A Wife in Musashino as a *ren'ai shōsetsu*, a love novel or romance, and there is almost no doubt that the enormous popularity of the novel rests on its melodramatic

[9] "*Musashino fujin no ito*" (My intentions in A Wife in Musashino), in Ōoka Shōhei shū, v. 15 (Tokyo: Iwanami shoten, 1982), p. 439.

and sentimental elements. Even so, the depiction of the nature of Michiko's love may be the most difficult aspect of the book for contemporary readers to comprehend. This is in part because the notion of romantic love, of love based on mutual attraction, carries enormous negative connotations for a woman like Michiko. As pleasant and natural as her feelings for Tsutomu are, she has been trained since childhood to view love as a passion that is potentially dangerous and certainly unbefitting a wife, because it is an expression of willfulness and emotional autonomy. In the case of her love for Tsutomu, which was both adulterous and incestuous, the emotion is destructive of all the things that create and sustain her identity: her status, family, and home. Seen in this light, Michiko's ambivalence is not just psychologically credible, but crucial to the design of the novel, in which the importance of place is an overriding concern. It is therefore significant that Michiko confronts her feelings for Tsutomu at the very heart of Musashino, at the source of the Nogawa in Koigakubo. Musashino confers meaning and identity on Michiko, but it also contains a place associated with tragic love that stirs her consciousness of conflicted emotions.

Michiko's strength of character is based on her capacity to feel deeply, a capacity she demonstrated by the doting attention she gave to her brothers and to Akiyama. Thus, she is able to feel genuine love for Tsutomu, but she is also strong enough to suppress that desire even while her husband is cheating on her. The turmoil in her heart is a threat to her sense of self, but so long as she remains in the place that provides her with spiritual stability she can defend her old-fashioned modesty. Her ability to protect herself crumbles away, however, when the second crisis arises. Akiyama, Tomiko, and Ōno all conspire in different ways to take Hake away from her. All their actions—the disposition of the Miyaji estate that gave Akiyama partial control; the way Akiyama and Tomiko flaunt their adultery; Ōno's misuse of Michiko's land for his business; Akiyama's demand for a divorce—are driven by selfish motives that take advantage of the changing legal and economic realities of the postwar. They not only put Michiko at a disadvantage, but also effectively diminish the value of her old-fashioned status as wife. The sympathy of the novel toward Michiko's loss of status gives evidence of more than just a little nostalgia; but this loss of status credibly explains her reasons for choosing to die. Michiko's death gives her the chance to redeem herself as wife, to balance the moral scales, and to show her love for Tsutomu. For his part, Akiyama misreads her motives as badly as he misreads Stendhal. In order to deflect blame from himself, he has to read Michiko's death as a romantic tragedy in which she sacrificed herself for Tsutomu. With no moral center himself, he is able neither to grasp the moral consciousness of Michiko, nor to understand that her motive for death is inextricably bound to her love and to her role as wife.

Michiko is the dominating presence of Ōoka's novel, but her cousin Tsutomu is in many ways the most interesting, disturbing, and heart-breaking of all the characters. Displaced as a boy by his parents' divorce, then as a young man by the trauma of battle, he is described by a bewildering range of contradictory characteristics: decadent, brutish, amoral, quiet, sensitive, and thoughtful. Tsutomu bears the scars of the war and desperately needs to be spiritually healed and emotionally comforted. His experience in the military has made him cynical and selfish, and yet at the same time it has given him powers of introspection that make him the most self-reflective character in the novel. He is capable of deluding himself and rationalizing his behavior, but he also has the capacity to judge himself in a cold and objective manner.

Although Tsutomu is out of place when he finally returns to Japan, he is the character most overtly associated with place because of his study of the topography of Musashino. Here we see one of the clearest links between this novel and *Fires on the Plain*. In *Fires on the Plain* the protagonist, Private Tamura, is forced to read the alien landscape of the Philippines not just to survive, but also to find a way to make whole again his fractured soul. In a similar manner, Tsutomu explores the native landscape of Musashino as a way to find himself. In the process of exploring the land, of seeking out meaning and identity in the ancient ground of Japanese culture, he discovers that Michiko is what he wants to be—a person rooted in a place, virtuous because she is grounded in an identity and in values that are authentic. The love he feels for her, and she for him, springs from this intense identification. As cousins their love is already incestuous; but the identification goes further in that they look like each other, like brother and sister. Their mutual passion amounts in effect to a kind of self-love in that they recognize in each other a Platonic ideal of themselves.

The identity Tsutomu sees in Michiko and the sense of belonging he feels when he is at Hake have been denied to him by the circumstances of his childhood and by the war. His love for Michiko brings him close to obtaining both, to obtaining peace for himself, but that is denied in the end by Michiko's moral consciousness, which demands that they separate. Her decision wounds him to the point of despair, which he expresses in violent fantasies of murdering every citizen of Tokyo by poisoning the water supply. Appalled by his own fantasy, he is caught in a downward spiral of longing, regret, and despair. When Michiko dies, Tsutomu undergoes a final displacement, a total exile. Ōno's news brings about such a complete destruction of meaning, feeling, and identity that Tsutomu is no longer human.

Tsutomu's fate is disturbing and moving, but Ōoka does not treat either the death of Michiko or Tsutomu's metamorphosis in the language of a love novel. His style throughout the work is dry and unsentimental, creating a voice that is distant and at times ironical. In this respect Ōoka openly acknowledged his debt to Stendhal and to Radiguet, whose style, Ōoka noted, had been compared to the dry reverberation of ivory on ivory caused by the movement of chess pieces across the board.[10] The

[10] Ibid., p. 439. The use of the image of chess pieces to describe Radiguet's style was suggested to Ōoka by Albert Thibaudet's 1938 study, *Reflections on the Novel*, which Ōoka cites in "*Musashino fujin no ito*."

rarefied elegance suggested by this image may apply in some degree to Ōoka, but that does not mean that the tone of the novel is aloof and emotionally detached. By questioning motives and foregrounding the historical and personal forces acting on his characters, Ōoka's style and narrative method gives them depth, bringing the reader closer to an affective understanding of the nature of the tragedy that befalls Michiko and Tsutomu.

Because the impact of a novel on the consciousness of its age is not quantifiable, it is easy to overestimate its critical value. By the same token, however, it is just as easy to underestimate its impact. *A Wife in Musashino* brings the postwar period in Japan to life through the enactment of a tragic tale that has universal resonance. The care and precision with which Ōoka depicts motivations and circumstances enables him to bring his story to the point where it gains an almost inexorable momentum. This is perhaps his greatest strength as a writer, and it is the basis for the lasting appeal of his fiction.

Acknowledgements

I have tried to recreate the clarity and spare elegance of Ōoka's original Japanese. This was not an easy task, and I am realistic enough to know that the phrase "partial success" is not so much an evaluative description as a synonym for translation. Because I am aware of my own limitations, I am genuinely grateful for all the help I have received in preparing this book. Jay Rubin and an anonymous reader from the Japanese Literature Publishing Project patiently and painstakingly corrected errors of fact and interpretation in an early draft of the manuscript, and they made valuable suggestions related to my rendering of Ōoka's narrative style and voice. Bruce Willoughby and James Hynes of the Center for Japanese Studies at the University of Michigan have been careful and insightful editors who have improved my work immeasurably. I am indebted to them both. Finally, I want to thank my wife and partner, Ikuko Watanabe, who assisted and supported my work at every stage in the preparation of the manuscript.

ABOUT THE TRANSLATOR

Dennis Washburn teaches Japanese and Comparative Literature at Dartmouth College. In addition to *A Wife in Musashino*, he has also translated Ōoka Shōhei's *The Shade of Blossoms* and Yokomitsu Riichi's *Shanghai* for the Center for Japanese Studies.